Thomas Schirrmacher

**Advocate of Love –
Martin Bucer
as Theologian and Pastor**

"World of Theology Series"

Studies published by the Theological Commission of the World Evangelical Alliance

Vol 5

Vol 1	Thomas K. Johnson: The First Step in Missions Training: How our Neighbors are Wrestling with God's General Revelation
Vol 2	Thomas K. Johnson: Christian Ethics in Secular Cultures
Vol 3	David Parker: Discerning the Obedience of Faith: A Short History of the World Evangelical Alliance Theological Commission
Vol 4	Thomas Schirrmacher (Ed.): William Carey: Theologian – Linguist – Social Reformer
Vol 5	Thomas Schirrmacher: Advocate of Love – Martin Bucer as Theologian and Pastor
Vol 6	Thomas Schirrmacher: Culture of Shame / Culture of Guilt
Vol 7	Thomas Schirrmacher: The Koran and the Bible
Vol 8	Thomas Schirrmacher (Ed.): The Humanisation of Slavery in the Old Testament
Vol 9	Jim Harries: New Foundations for Appreciating Africa: Beyond Religious and Secular Deceptions
Vol 10	Thomas Schirrmacher: Missio Dei – God's Missional Nature
Vol 11	Thomas Schirrmacher: Biblical Foundations for 21st Century World Mission

Theologisches Lehr- und Studienmaterial (Martin Bucer Seminar)

Vol 30

In selection:

Vol 4	Henry Krabbendam – Sovereignty and Responsibility
Vol 9	Henry Krabbendam – James: A Practical Commentary
Vol 11	John Warwick Montgomery – Tractatus Logico-Theologicus
Vol 18	Johannes Calvin – Institutio
Vol 19	Eduard Böhl – Dogmatik
Vol 20	Thomas Schirrmacher – Scham- oder Schuldgefühl?
Vol 21	Cambron Teupe – Einführung in das neutestamentliche Griechisch
Vol 22	David Garrison – Gemeindegründungs-Bewegungen
Vol 23	Carsten Friedrich – Die Schatten der himmlischen Dinge: Typologie im Hebräerbrief
Vol 24	Franz Graf-Stuhlhofer – „Das Ende naht!"
Vol 25	Bodo Heller – Das Reich Gottes zwischne Annahme und Ablehnung
Vol 26	Franz Graf-Stuhlhofer – Christliche Bücher kritisch lesen
Vol 27	Margarita Heller – ‚Er offenbarte seine Herrlichkeit': Kommentar zu Johannes 1-4
Vol 28	Christoph Jung – Da waren's nur noch neun ... Das Sabbatgebot und die Christen
Vol 29	Wayne Grudem – Biblische Dogmatik
Vol 30	Thomas Schirrmacher – Advocate of Love – Martin Bucer as Theologian and Pastor
Vol 31	Daniel Dangendorf – Musikethik in der Gemeinde
Vol 32:	Titus Vogt – Von Ewigkeit erwählt?!
Vol 34:	To Be Continued: A 21st Century Update of the Heidelberg Catechism of the Christian Church from North Central Java
Vol 35:	Frank Hinkelmann. GOTT*esdienst* feiern – Geschichte, Theologie und Praxis des christlichen Gottesdienstes – Ein Kompendium
Vol 36:	Daniel Facius – ICH BIN Die Selbstoffenbarung Jesu in den Bildreden des Joh.-Ev.

Thomas Schirrmacher

Advocate of Love – Martin Bucer as Theologian and Pastor

Achieving Unity through Listening to the Scriptures and to Each Other

Martin Bucer's Theological and Practical Agenda as a Challenge to Evangelicals Today

Translated by Richard McClary

Edited by Thomas K. Johnson

WIPF & STOCK · Eugene, Oregon

Wipf and Stock Publishers
199 W 8th Ave, Suite 3
Eugene, OR 97401

Advocate of Love
Martin Bucer as Theologian and Pastor
By Schirrmacher, Thomas
Copyright©2013 Verlag für Kultur und Wissenschaft
ISBN 13: 978-1-5326-5543-2
Publication date 4/12/2018
Previously published by Verlag für Kultur und Wissenschaft, 2013

Contents

Bucer and Evangelicals 9
The unknown Bucer 9
Martin Bucer (resumé in tabular form) 12
Building Christ's Kingdom 20
Theologian of the Holy Spirit 21
The Inspiration of God's Word 22
Ethics as Sanctification Arising Out of Justification 23
Bucer and the Law 26
Learning from the Anabaptists 27
Confirmation 31
Pastoral Care as a Sign of Jesus' Church 33
Church Discipline 35
Lay Elders 37
Christian Communities 38
The Meaning of the Family in the Church Community 43
Apologetics and the Priesthood of Believers 44
The Pietist among the Reformers 45
The Puritan among the Reformers 47
Bucer wanted Christian Unity 48
Unity through Truth 51
Thoughts about Election 53
Domiciled in the Reformed Camp 54
Calvin became a Calvinist through Bucer 55
Exegesis Is Prior to Dogmatics 58
A Theology of Love 58
Unity and the Lord's Supper 59
The Cologne Reformation 61
The Role of the Church Fathers 63
Bucer Was Internationally Active 64
A Proponent of World Missions Not Befitting His Time 66
The Influence of His Liturgy 67
Bucer's Social Ethic 69
A Critical Partner of the State 70
Groundbreaking and Innovative Ethics in Detail 74
Marriage Is a Love Partnership 74
A New View of Divorce 76
The Tragedy of the Bigamy of Philipp von Hessen 78
Bucer as a Role Model for Our Time 80
A Discussion of Three New Important Dissertations on Martin Bucer 80
About the Author 89

"Bucer? That slick rogue (what a treat) . . ." (Martin Luther on Martin Bucer)[1]

"In the true knowledge of God one only knows as much as one can bring to expression in his own life."[2]
(Martin Bucer)

"No one wants to learn. Everyone [wants] to teach."[3]
"Every person should accept the speech of another as if it was spoken to promote the truth, to then think about which truth could be in such speech, as faithfully as one can, so that what is said becomes real."[4]
(Martin Bucer on conversations among Christians)

"If one wants to immediately judge someone as deserted by the Spirit of Christ just because an individual does not judge the same as oneself, and if one is prepared to go after someone as an enemy of the truth because that person might hold something false for true, then whom can one still look upon as a brother? I have personally never seen two people who think exactly the same thing. And that also applies to theology."
(Martin Bucer, 1530, in the preface to his commentary on the Gospels)

"The former Dominican monk Martin Bucer (1491-1551) . . . deserves a place next to the great Reformers such as Luther and Calvin for the strength of his thought and action."[5]

"During this time [1534] he became . . . one of the leading, if not the central figure, at least within German Protestantism."[6]

"Bucer is of great importance for institutions of the Evangelical church. He achieved this via the documents he composed for various German territories and imperial cities concerning church order. As they were communicated by Calvin, they shaped the entirety of Reformed Protestantism. Beyond that, he was indefatigable as he endeavored to achieve understanding among Protestants as well as understanding with the Catholic Church, such that his writings are of interest for present day

---

[1] Quoted from Gottfried Hammann. Martin Bucer. Gestalten des Protestantismus von gestern und heute. Christliches Verlags-Haus: Stuttgart, 1989. p. 25.
[2] Martin Bucer, quoted by Marijn de Kroon. Martin Bucer und Johannes Calvin. Vandenhoeck & Ruprecht: Göttingen, 1991. p. 242.
[3] Martin Bucer, quoted ibid., p. 238.
[4] Martin Bucer, quoted ibid., p. 239.
[5] Bernard Cottret. Calvin: Eine Biographie. Quell: Stuttgart, 1998. p. 165.
[6] Martin Greschat. Martin Bucer: Ein Reformator und seine Zeit. C. H. Beck: München, 1990. p. 143.

ecumenical discussions. He even took the inquiries from representatives of the so-called 'left wing' of the Reformation seriously. His efforts relating to the introduction of confirmation and church discipline were widely accepted. And he made basic contributions having to do with the relationship between church and state. On the one hand, he represented the freedom of the church and free church considerations. On the other hand, however, during his activities in Cambridge he laid the foundation for the English state church."[7]

"Under the conviction that 'being a Christian' always has to be lived in community, Bucer strove after sanctification, so that Christ was recognized in individual life as well as corporate life as Lord and Master."[8]

"In the process he was inexhaustibly active, regularly and indefatigably as a matter of course until deep into the night. The humanist and theologian Petrus Martyr Vermigli (1500-1562), who was driven out of Italy and who lived several years in Strasbourg, wrote in 1542: 'I have never seen Bucer inactive, either he is preaching or he is involved in organizing and leading the church [...]. After he has spent the day with such pursuits, he turns around and spends the night in study and prayer. Seldom have I ever awakened to find that he himself was not still awake.'"[9]

---

[7] Introduction on Bucer by the European Bucer research center at the University of Heidelberg (quoted on www.uni-heidelberg.de/institute/sonst/adw/bucer/vita.html – 29.9.2001).

[8] Reinhold Friedrich. „Martin Bucer". pp. 85-101 in: Christian Möller (ed.). Geschichte der Seelsorge in Einzelporträts. vol. 2. Von Martin Luther bis Matthias Claudius. Vandenhoeck & Ruprecht: Göttingen, 1995. p. 87.

[9] Martin Greschat. Martin Bucer. op. cit., p. 211.

Bucer and Evangelicals

Evangelicals comprise a worldwide movement that spans practically all denominations and even most confessions. Evangelicals are found on both sides of mainline, traditional churches and the newer small or revival churches. Thus the evangelical alliance in Germany early bridged the deep ditch between the German State Church and the free churches. Evangelicals bridge Reformed theology and more recent theological developments while also connecting traditional structures with all sorts of revivalist movements.

That is reason enough to take the Reformer, who embodied all of this already in the 16th century, as a role model: Martin Bucer from Strassbourg. This is not to make an Evangelical out of Bucer or to redirect his stream towards the Evangelical mill, just as little as anyone should talk Bucer up as the one exemplary Christian. Nevertheless, Bucer represents the attempt to use Scripture to find what is common at a time when Christianity was experiencing fragmentation and to win back erring brothers in a manner that was both friendly and serious.

For *Martin Bucer European School of Theology and Research Institutes*, the institution I lead and which made the following research possible, Bucer is more than just someone who accidentally provides us with the seminary's name; for one and one-half years he preached and wrote in the vicinity of our Bonn Study Center as the Reformation was initiated.

Reformed and reforming, yet open to hear all voices from within Christendom, whether it was in conversation with Lutherans, Baptists or spiritualists, Bucer truly desired Christian unity. However, he did not want unity at the cost of biblical theology or reduced conviction. Rather, Bucer persued unity by working in a concerted manner with Scripture and by working on basic theological convictions.

In our opinion, that is the order of the day for Christians and Evangelicals, and it is also the task of a theological seminary: to clearly work out the non-negotiable basics anew and to defend them, to simultaneously identify which questions are less important, and by listening to others to always rethink things together with open Bibles.

The unknown Bucer

For a long time Bucer was the least known of the great Reformers. Heinrich Bornkamm calls Bucer, alongside Luther and Melanchthon, the 'third

German Reformer,'[10] whereby among the great Reformers in Imperial Germany he was the only non-Lutheran and rather reformed Reformer. He achieved this status without establishing a denomination and without possessing the covert teaching authority associated with a movement.

The absence of a tradition associated with his name produced a lack of interest in him.[11] There are Lutherans, Calvinists, and Mennonites, but there are no 'Bucerians.' That could be the reason why it was not until 1952 that a German-French working group began overseeing a not yet finished, new edition of Bucer writings since 1954/1955.[12] Most of the writings are still available as originals, not, however, in modern German, English, or French versions or translations.

Since at an older age Bucer was controversial during his time in Strasbourg, it was not possible in the 16th century to release a complete edition of writings. Bucer lived on in the consciences of most researchers simply through his Genevan student, John Calvin. Bucer was gradually rediscovered in the 19th century by historians and not by theologians. Modern Bu-

---

[10] Heinrich Bornkamm. „Martin Bucer: Der dritte deutsche Reformator" (1952). pp. 88-112 in: ders. Das Jahrhundert der Reformation. Vandenhoeck & Ruprecht: Göttingen, 1961; affirmed in Gottfried Hammann. „Die ekklesiologischen Hintergründe zur Bildung von Bucers 'Christlichen Gemeinschaften' in Straßburg (1546-1548)". Zeitschrift für Kirchengeschichte 105 (1994): 344-360, here p. 275.

[11] In part. Heinrich Bornkamm. Martin Bucers Bedeutung für die europäische Reformationsgeschichte. op. cit., p. 36.

[12] From the collected works 'Martini Buceri Opera Omnia' the following have appeared up till now: Series 1 (German) 1-7, 9-11, 17 (vol. 6 has three sub-volumes), Series 2 (Latin) 1-5, 15 (2 volumes), Series 3 (letters) 1-4 + register volume 3a. In 1958 the German Research Foundation started an edition of German writings of Martin Bucer in Münster, which was taken over in 1980 by the Heidelberger Academy of Sciences and Humanities. It has had its headquarters in Heidelberg since 1994. It is a branch of the international project for the first historico-critical complete edition of Bucer's works. Latin works are published by the theological faculty of the University of Strasbourg with the inclusion of an international team of editors. Six volumes have appeared up until now. The publication of Bucer's correspondence (DFG Project) is located at the University of Erlangen. Of the close to 3000 letters, around 350 have been published in the four volumes that are now available. The annotated edition of Martin Bucer's German writings presently consists of eleven volumes. Ten additional volumes are anticipated. On the basis of its extensiveness it will be an undertaking that will last approximately an additional 20. Compare to these efforts Gottfried Seebaß. „Bucer-Forschung seit dem Jubiläumsjahr 1991". Theologische Rundschau 62 (1997): 271-300, pp. 277-282 and Andreas Gäummann. Reich Christi und Obrigkeit: Eine Studie zum reformatorischen Denken und Handeln Martin Bucers. Zürcher Beiträge zur Reformationsgeschichte 20. Peter Lang: Bern, 2001. pp. 36-38.

cer research did not really begin until his 400th birthday in 1891.[13] Since that time, literature about Bucer has steadily grown,[14] and today there are also many good expositions in German,[15] even if succinct German collections of Bucer's texts are a long time coming.

---

[13] The complete paragraph according to Robert Stupperich. „Bucer, Martin". pp. 258-270 in: Gerhard Müller (ed.). Theologische Realenzyklopädie. vol. 7. de Gruyter: Berlin, 1981/1993 (study edition). p. 267.

[14] Works about Bucer are recorded in the following biographies up to 1951: Robert Stupperich. Bibliographia Bucerana. Schriften des Vereins für Reformationsgeschichte Nr. 169 (volume 58, issue 2). C. Bertelsmann: Gütersloh, 1952. 95 pp. [together with Heinrich Bornkamm. Martin Bucers Bedeutung für die europäische Reformationsgeschichte]; 1951-1974: Mechthild Köhn. „Bucer-Bibliographie 1951-1974". pp. 138-165 in: Marijn de Kroon et al. (ed.). Bucer und seine Zeit: Forschungsbeiträge und Bibliographie. Veröffentlichungen des Instituts für Europäische Geschichte Mainz 80. Steiner: Wiesbaden, 1976; 1975-1998: Thomas Wilhelmi et al. „Bucer-Bibliographie 1975-1998". Travaux de la Faculté de Strasbourg 9. Assoc. des Publ. de la Fac. Théologie Protestante; Strasbourg, 1999. A complete bibliography with a directory of all publications relating to Bucer which have been received is being prepared. See www.uni-heidelberg.de/institute/sonst/adw/bucer/biblio.html (29.9.2001). Also comp. Gottfried Seebaß. „Bucer-Forschung seit dem Jubiläumsjahr 1991". Theologische Rundschau 62 (1997): 271-300 and the excellent presentation of the most important research contributions in Andreas Gäumann. Reich Christi und Obrigkeit. op. cit., p. 21-32.

[15] The two best complete studies are, in my opinion Martin Greschat. Martin Bucer: Ein Reformator und seine Zeit. C. H. Beck: München, 1990 and Gottfried Hammann. Martin Bucer: 1491-1551. Zwischen Volkskirche und Bekenntnisgemeinschaft. Veröffentlichungen des Instituts für Europäische Geschichte 139. Steiner: Stuttgart, 1989 (French original Entre la secte e la cite, 1984) [The first part is geared towards biographical information.] With a clearly arranged outline: Gottfried Hammann (diagrams: Pierre Léon Dupuis, Max Roubinet). Martin Bucer. Gestalten des Protestantismus von gestern und heute. Christliches Verlags-Haus: Stuttgart, 1989. 52 pp.] and Andreas Gäumann. Reich Christi und Obrigkeit: Eine Studie zum reformatorischen Denken und Handeln Martin Bucers. Zürcher Beiträge zur Reformationsgeschichte 20. Peter Lang: Bern, 2001. Additionally, the following complete overviews and essay collections are recommended: Marijn de Kroon, Friedhelm Krüger (ed.). Bucer und seine Zeit. Veröffentlichungen des Instituts für Europäische Geschichte 80. Steiner: Wiesbaden, 1976 (pp. 138-165 Quellen und Literatur 1951-1974); Hastings Eells. Martin Bucer. Russell & Russell: New York, 1971 (1931 reprint); Hartmut Joisten. Der Grenzgänger Martin Bucer: Ein deutscher Reformator. Ev. Presseverlag Pfalz: Speyer, 1991; Heinrich Bornkamm. Martin Bucers Bedeutung für die europäische Reformationsgeschichte. Schriften des Vereins für Reformationsgeschichte No. 169 (volume 58, issue 2). C. Bertelsmann: Gütersloh, 1952. 36 pp.; Werner Neuser. „Von Zwingli und Calvin bis zur Synode von Westminster". Werner Neuser. „Von Zwingli und Calvin bis zur Synode von Westminster". pp. 167-352 in: Carl Andresen (ed.). Handbuch der Dogmen- und Theologiegeschichte 2. Vandenhoeck & Ruprecht: Göttin-

We find ourselves at a time when the question of the unity of the church of Jesus Christ is again of interest, and in particular when a question moving the Evangelical world is how, among the underbrush of different theological outlooks, we can separate basic teaching and values in our faith from second order questions. This means there is great significance attached to a Reformer, who for his entire life did not let himself be categorized into a particular denomination, who spoke and discussed with everyone, whether they were Lutheran, Reformed, Anabaptist or spiritualist, and who also never tired of bringing Christians together.

Martin Bucer (resumé in tabular form)

November 11, 1491	(Martinmas) Born in the free imperial city of Schlettstadt (Sélestat) and attended Latin school (grammar school) in Schlettstadt until 1507
1507	Becomes a Dominican Monk in Schlettstadt
approx. 1510-14	Studied logic within the religious order
1515-1516	Two-year introduction to the study of theology in Heidelberg und Mainz
1516	Ordained as a priest in Mainz
1517-1520	Study of liberal arts in Heidelberg as part of obtaining the degree of doctor of theology (he did not obtain the degree, since he fled the monastery in 1520)
April 1518	Participates in the Heidelberg Disputation and gets to know Luther there; becomes 'Evangelical'
1519	Bucer receives bachelor of arts and master's degrees
Summer of 1519	In the course of a disputation, Bucer for the first time defends his new theological convictions

---

gen, 1989 (Nachdruck von 1980). pp. 209-224; Robert Stupperich. „Bucer, Martin". op. cit.; Christian Krieger, Marc Lienhard (ed.). Martin Bucer and Sixteenth Century Europe. vol. 1. Studies in Medieval and Reformation Thought 52. Brill: Leiden, 1993; Christian Krieger, Marc Lienhard (ed.). Martin Bucer and Sixteenth Century Europe. vol. 2. Studies in Medieval and Reformation Thought 53. Brill: Leiden, 1993; Comp. also a complete overview of Bucer's ethics and Bucer's ecclesiology, which are compiled in the text.

1520	The leitmotiv of Bucer's theology becomes crystallized: the unity of justification with the gift of a new and better Christian life through the gift of the Spirit
November 1520	Flees the monastery
February 1521	Bucer moves to Ebernburg and is taken in by Franz von Sickingen; works as Ulrich von Hutten's right-hand man
April 1521	Released from the vows of the religious order and becomes a Diocesan Priest
May 1521	Becomes court chaplain for the Palatine Count Friedrich in Bruchsal and attends Imperial Diets in Worms and Nuremberg
August 1521	Bucer in New Market in the Bavarian Upper Palatinate
May 1522	Franz von Sickingen confers the parish of Landstuhl upon Bucer
Summer 1522	Attention-getting marriage to the nun Elizabeth Silbereisen (died in 1541) in Landstuhl – one of the first marriages of a priest at the time of the Reformation
November 1522	Driven out in the chaos of war; spends a short time as pastor in Wîssembourg in the Alsace
February 1523	Excommunicated by the Bishop of Speyer
April 1523	Bucer's disputation in Wîssembourg regarding his rejection of ecclesiastical ceremonies
May 1523	Flees once more due to Franz von Sickingen's defeat; taken in at the house of the adherent of the Reformation movement, Matthew Zell, in Strasbourg
August 1523	Important first writings with a presentation of Bucer's theology 'Das ym selbs niemant, sondern anderen leben soll, und wie der mensch dahin kummen mög' (That no one lives for himself, but that rather one should live for others, and how an individual can do so)
End of 1523	Official commencement of the Reformation in Strasbourg

March 1524	Pastor in Strasbourg; the peasant farmers make Bucer their pastor at St. Aurelia with the approval of the city council
September 1524	Karlstadt the spiritualist comes to Strasbourg
September 1524	Bucer finally becomes a citizen of Strasbourg
December 1524	'Grund und ursach …', the major defense of Strasbourg's Reformation
1525	Production of an Evangelical order of worship with Bucer's cooperation
1525	Start of the Protestant controversy regarding the Lord's Supper
1525	Peasants' War; Bucer und Capito are unable to prevent war in the Alsace
1526	Droves of refugees come to Strasbourg, among them many Anabaptists and spiritualists
May 1526	Bucer produces an expert opinion for the council of the city of Strasbourg
1526	Introduction of catechism lessons for children as called for by Bucer
End of 1526	First disputations with Anbaptist leaders together with Capito in Strasbourg
February 1526	Abolishment of the Mass in Strasbourg
June 1527	'Getrewe Warnung' ('Faithful Warning') regarding Anabaptists
1527	Bucer's first Bible commentary appears – covers the four Gospels and Paul's Letter to the Ephesians
January 1528	Bucer participates in the Bern Disputation, which leads to the introduction of the Reformation in Bern
January 1528	Bucer gets to know Zwingli personally, with whom he had corresponded by letter since 1523
1528	„Vergleichung D. Luthers und seins gegentheyls vom Abentmal Christi. Dialogus, Das ist eyn freündtlich gesprech" ("A comparison and contrast of Luther and the Lord's Supper of Christ. A dialogue, or friendly discussion") In this Bucer attempts to achieve an understanding with Martin Luther and the Lutherans

1529-1540	Bucer becomes pastor of the influential St. Thomas Church in Strasbourg
October 1529	Bucer participates in the Colloquy of Marburg in an attempt to resolve the controversy over the Lord's Supper
1530	Bucer produces a massive commentary on the Gospels ('Enarrationes perpetuae in sacra quatuor evangelia')
June 1530	Bucer and Capito compose a 'Confession Tetrapolitana' (confession of four cities) for Strasbourg, Memmingen, Constance and Lindau (and later Ulm)
1530	Bucer meets Luther in the Coburg und first dispels Luther's distrust for Oberdeutsche (Upper Germans)
1530	Journey through Upper Germany and Switzerland in order to awaken a readiness for mutual rapprochement
July 1530	Bucer conducts discussions in Augsburg with Brenz und Brück regarding the Lord's Supper
September 1530	Bucer again visits Luther
October 1530	Bucer visits Zwingli in Zurich ('shuttle diplomacy')
November 1530	Alliance between Swiss cities and Strasbourg with Hessen
February 1531	Zwingli breaks from Bucer
1531	Bucer achieves the admittance of Upper German cities and Strasbourg into the Schmalkaldic Federation
1531	With Zwingli's death (1531), Bucer is recognized as the head of Upper German Protestants
1531	Bucer functions decidedly on site in Ulm, Memmingen, and Biberach to implement the Reformation
1531	First appointment of lay elders (church wardens) in Strasbourg upon Bucer's request
End of 1531	Renewed disputation between Bucer and Anabaptist leaders
August 1532	„Vom mangel der religion, an deren alles hanget" ("Of a lack of religion upon which everything de-

	pends") produced regarding the necessity of holding discussions with sectarians
April/May 1533	Bucer visits Basel and Zurich
June 1533	First synod in Strasbourg – Decree and introduction of Bucer's liturgy; additional decree on church discipline – however, the city council delays for a long period of time and then only implements a portion of the decree
September 1533	With his "urbereytung zum Concilio" ("counciliar revision") Bucer promotes a collective German council
October 1533	Second meeting of the Strasbourg synod – the adoption of church order marks the high point of Bucer's influence in Strasbourg
1533	Bucer also becomes praeses (chairman) of the church synod
1534	Supports the Reformation in Wurttemberg
May 1534	Bucer produces his "The Larger Catechism"
December 1534	Count Philipp of Hessen calls Bucer to Kassel, where he comes to an agreement with Melanchthon on the issue of the Lord's Supper
1534/1535	Bucer assists in the implementation of the Reformation in Ulm and Augsburg
1534-37	Bucer plays a central role in ordering church communities in Augsburg
December 1534	Renewed detailed discussions with Melanchthon in Kassel
Mai 1536	Bucer organizes a conference in Wittenberg, at which he achieves the most significant agreement within all of evangelicalism, the "Wittenberg Concord," which Luther also approves
1536	By agreeing upon the "Wittenberg Concord," Bucer prevents the dissolution of the Schmalkaldic Federation
1536	Commentary on Paul's Letter to the Romans – Bucer's exegetical magnum opus

1534	Supports the Reformation in Benfeld
1538	Founds the Strasbourg secondary school; Johannes Sturm becomes the headmaster
1538	Produces „Von der waren Seelsorge" ("On the true care of souls"), a comprehensive doctrine of care of souls and pastoral theology
1538-1541	Calvin in Strasbourg
October	December 1538 – Bucer conducts discussions in Marburg with Marburg Anabaptists
December 1538	Bucer's recommended anti-Jewish policy for Hessen
1539	Integration of Anabaptists in Hessen through Bucer's Ziegenhain Order of Discipline and Kassel Church Order (1539), in particular by admitting church discipline and confirmation
Jan 1539	Bucer participates in religious discussions in Leipzig
May 1539	Second Strasbourg Synod – The council rejects most demands
June 1539	Unification efforts commence via Bucer's 'Nürnberger fridestand' (Nuremberg Peace Accord)
End of 1539	Bucer allows Philipp of Hessen's bigamy
At the turn of the year 1539/1540	Bucer attends Leipzig religious discussions in connection with the introduction of the Reformation in the Dukedom of Saxony
March 1540	Philipp of Hessen enters into bigamous marital relationship
Mid-1540	Bucer participates in religious discussions in Hagenau
At the turn of the year 1540/1541	Bucer participates in religious discussions in Worms
1541	Bucer participates in religious discussion in Regensburg; a formula for unification ('Regensburg Book') is co-composed by Bucer
1541	Bucer conducts secret talks with the Catholic theologian Johannes Gropper and Protestant princes; these talks later broke down

November 1541	Bucer's first wife and all Bucer's children, as well as Wolfgang Capito, die from the plague
1541	Bucer becomes Superintendent of the Strasbourg church after Capito's death and a member of the chapter of St Thomas church
February 1542	First meeting with Johannes Gropper and the Archbishop of Cologne Hermann of Wied regarding the questions of reform in the archdiocese
April 1542	Bucer marries Capito's widow Wibrandis Rosenblatt (who survives him)
December 1542	Bucer moves to Bonn, the political capital of the Archdiocese of Cologne and preaches regularly in Münster
1542	Bucer supports the Reformation in Metz
1542	Bucer supports the Reformation in Frankfurt
1542-1543	Archbishop Hermann von Wied's Cologne Reformation under Bucer's Leadership
Mai 1543	Melanchthon spends time in Bonn to support Bucer. Together they compose the major document of the Cologne Reformation – "Simple Objections" („Einfältige Bedenken")
1543	Supports Reformation efforts in the Archdiocese of Trier
1543	After the defeat of Protestants in the Schmalkaldic War, a movement begins to re-catholicize the Archdiocese of Cologne
1543	Bohemian Brethren print Bucer's work on the care of souls in Czech
1544	Bucer becomes superintendent of the chapter of St. Thomas Church in Strasbourg
1544-48	Supports the Reformation in the Electoral Palatinate (Kurpfalz)
1545	Supports the Reformation in Hamburg
April 1546	Hermann von Wied is removed from the position of archbishop, whereby the Cologne Reformation definitively founders

1545/46	Bucer participates in religious discussions in Regensburg
1545-48	Supports the Reformation in Grafschaft Hanau-Lichtenberg
1547-49	In Strasbourg Bucer organizes 'Christian Communities' ('Christliche Gemeinschaften'), a type of core house church, which increasingly arouses the resistance of the council
March 1547	Strasbourg submits to the Emperor in the Schmalkaldic War
October 1547	Strasbourg's council forbids pastors from all measures that serve to establish church discipline
November 1547	The council forbids 'Christian Communities' ('Christliche Gemeinschaften')
April/May 1548	The Augsburg Interim issues and includes only limited concessions to Protestants – Bucer declines to give his signature in Augsburg, is detained, signs, and is released.
July 1548	In his "A Summary Mistake of Christian Teaching and Religion" („Ein Summarischer vergriff der Christlichen Lehre vnd religion"), Bucer condemns the Augsburger Interim and becomes the leader of the opposition party; conflict arises thereby with the council of the city of Strasbourg
February 1549	Strasbourg concedes to an imperial ultimatum
March 1549	Bucer is relieved of all offices in Strasbourg and leaves the city under pressure by the Emperor
April 1549	Bucers flees to England, following the call of Archbishop Thomas Cranmer of Canterbury to assist in Edward VI's Reformation efforts; initially he lives in Cranmer's London residence, Lambeth Palace, and then in his summer house 30 kilometers from London
December 1549	Bucer receives a doctorate of theology and becomes a professor at Cambridge
January 1550	Produces an opinion on the first version of Anglican liturgy, the Book of Common Prayer

October 1550	Bucer's last large work "De regno Christi" is produced for the English king, including a comprehensive program of church and societal reform
February 28, 1551	Bucer dies in Cambridge
February 1556	Heresy proceedings against Bucer are conducted under the Catholic Queen Mary; his corpse and his writings are publicly burned
July 1560	Officially rehabilitated by Queen Elizabeth; this action was accompanied by ceremonial dedication of his grave and a memorial in Cambridge

Building Christ's Kingdom

Bucer wanted "all areas of life to be placed under the lordship of Christ,"[16] because the Kingdom of God meant nothing more and nothing less to him.[17]

> "From its beginnings in Strasbourg to its end in Cambridge (this is demonstrated by writings from 1523, „Das ym selb ..." and 1551, „De Regno Christi"), Bucer's theology circled around the idea of implementing God's or Christ's lordship in the world."[18]

However, the kingdom of God extends itself only by the power of the Holy Spirit. It does this on a small scale in the life of each individual and on a large scale in the church and the state. "The kingdom of God exercises its lordship here on earth by the Holy Spirit's work in believers."[19]

---

[16] Martin Greschat. Martin Bucer. op. cit., p. 246.
[17] No one has worked this out more soundly than Andreas Gäumann. Reich Christi und Obrigkeit. op. cit. pp. 131-135 (with almost all quoted references for the expression Kingdom of Christ, or *Reich Christi,* in his works) and p. 159 and the entire book.
[18] Reinhold Friedrich. Martin Bucer – 'Fanatiker der Einheit'? Diss.: Neuchatel, 1990. p. 195. The information regarding Bucers last book as an old man *De regno* is found further below. The early work 'Das ym selbs niemant, sonder anderen leben soll, und wie der mensch dahyn kummen mög' are found in Martin Bucer. Die Frühschriften 1520-1524. ed. by Robert Stupperich. Martini Buceri Opera Omnia, Series I: Deutsche Schriften. vol. 1. Gütersloher Verlagshaus: Gütersloh & Presses Universitaires de France: Paris, 1960. pp. 29-67.
[19] Karl Koch. Studium Pietatis: Martin Bucer als Ethiker. Beiträge zur Geschichte und Lehre der Reformierten Kirche 14. Neukirchener Verlag: Neukirchen, 1962. p. 51.

Theologian of the Holy Spirit

For this reason, August Lang[20] called Bucer the theologian of the Spirit.[21] Actually, Bucer's emphasis on pneumatology[22] with respect to the life of a Christian as well as with respect to ecclesiology[23] is one of his prominent characteristics. At most Calvin can 'keep up' with Bucer in this respect.[24] Bucer's teaching on the Holy Spirit "leads us into the heart of the theology of the Holy Spirit."[25]

Various authors have recognized that Bucer gives the Holy Spirit its central New Testament position. "For all of Bucer's theology, the position and activity of the Spirit is foundational."[26]

---

[20] August Lang. Der Evangelienkommentar Martin Butzers und die Grundzüge seiner Theologie. Studien zur Geschichte der Theologie und der Kirche 2,2. Dieterich: Leipzig, 1900; Nachdruck Scientia: Aalen, 1972. pp. 120-123; comp. August Lang. Puritanismus und Pietismus: Studien zu ihrer Entwicklung von M. Butzer bis zum Methodismus. Buchhandlung des Erziehungsvereins: Neukirchen, 1941. pp. 13-71 („Butzer und der Puritanismus").

[21] Compare as most extensive W. Peter Stephens. The Holy Spirit in the Theology of Martin Bucer. University Press: Cambridge, 1970; Yoon-Bae Choi. De verhouding tussen pneumatologie en christologie bij Martin Bucer en Johannes Calvijn. Groen: Leiden, 1996 und L. G. Zwanenburg. „Martin Bucer over de Heilige Geest". Theologia Reformatat 8 (1965): 105-129; Willem van't Spijker. „Die Lehre vom Heiligen Geist bei Bucer und Calvin". pp. 73-106 in: Wilhelm H. Neuser. Calvinus Servus Christi. Ráday-ollegium: Budapest, 1988; see also H. J. Selderhuis. „Die hermeneutisch-theologische Grundlage der Auffassungen Bucers zur Ehescheidung". pp. 229-243 in: Willem van't Spijker (ed.). Calvin: Erbe und Auftrag: Festschrift für Wilhelm Heinrich Neuser zum 65. Geburtstag. Kok: Kampen, 1991. pp. 241-243 and Andreas Gäumann. Reich Christi und Obrigkeit. op. cit., pp. 156-158.

[22] Also Werner Neuser. „Von Zwingli und Calvin bis zur Synode von Westminster". op. cit., p. 224.

[23] Comp. ibid. and Gottfried Hammann. Martin Bucer. op. cit., pp. 91-95 „Die Kirche als Werk des Heiligen Geistes."

[24] Comp. Willem van't Spijker. „Die Lehre vom Heiligen Geist bei Bucer und Calvin". pp. 73-106 in: Wilhelm H. Neuser. Calvinus Servus Christi. Ráday-Collegium: Budapest, 1988 und Yoon-Bae Choi. De verhouding tussen pneumatologie en christologie bij Martin Bucer en Johannes Calvijn. op. cit.

[25] Willem van't Spijker. „Die Lehre vom Heiligen Geist bei Bucer und Calvin". op. cit., p. 73. Ibid. p. 75 he assumes as does Stephens that there are "many keys" to Bucer's theology, but that the teaching on the Holy Spirit is one of the most important. However, according to p. 76 this teaching is at the same time completely "christologically determined."

[26] H. J. Selderhuis. „Die hermeneutisch-theologische Grundlage der Auffassungen Bucers zur Ehescheidung". op. cit., p. 242.

The Holy Spirit also determines all of Bucer's teaching on church community. "The Holy Spirit is the highest principle for church life. He allows the church to be established over the chosen,"[27] for which reason the Holy Spirit, and not human church leadership, always has the last word in and over the church.[28]

> "Even if Bucer pushed Christ to the center, as did the other Reformers, his thoughts circled more intensely around an understanding of the Holy Spirit. Bucer came nowhere close to Martin Luther in thinking deeply about what the cross of Christ, his suffering, and his death, means for each individual Christian and for his faith. For the Strasbourg Reformer, the cross was little more than a type of necessary and preliminary stage[29] prior to that new world free of pain and suffering, the representative and advocate of which is the resurrected one. From this new world, the Holy Spirit, according to Bucer's understanding, is active in the present, making people believers, working meaningfully in them, giving them courage, hope, and strength so that they might truly express brotherly love. Martin Bucer gained these insights through being continually occupied with the Holy Scriptures. From the Dominican monastery in Schlettstadt to the University in Cambridge, his life was a single bible study. The 'radiant divine word' was his highest authority, and it was the source and standard for his convictions."[30]

The Inspiration of God's Word

Bucer's understanding of the Scriptures is also completed influenced by pneumatology, and for that reason it is above all influenced by the teaching of inspiration.[31] Even if human and historical development of the Bible is taken very seriously and taken into account in interpretation, it is the Holy Spirit who is the actual author of the Scriptures. Since word and spirit be-

---

[27] Gottfried Hammann. Martin Bucer. op. cit., p. 91.
[28] Ibid. p. 92; comp. in part. W. Peter Stephens for the relationship between the Holy Spirit and the church. The Holy Spirit in the Theology of Martin Bucer. op. cit., pp. 156-166.
[29] That this judgment was not warranted becomes clear in the section on justification further below.
[30] Hartmut Joisten. Der Grenzgänger Martin Bucer. op. cit., pp. 163-164.
[31] Comp. in part. Johannes Müller. Martin Bucers Hermeneutik. Quellen und Forschungen zur Reformationsgeschichte 32. Mohn: Gütersloh, 1965. pp. 72-80; W. Peter Stephens. The Holy Spirit in the Theology of Martin Bucer. op. cit., pp. 129-155; Gottfried Hammann. Martin Bucer. op. cit., pp. 103-105 and 151-159 and Karl Koch. Studium Pietatis: Martin Bucer als Ethiker. Beiträge zur Geschichte und Lehre der Reformierten Kirche 14. Neukirchener Verlag: Neukirchen, 1962. pp. 29-30.

long together,[32] the Holy Spirit plays not only a leading role in the development of the Scriptures, but also plays a leading role so that the Scriptures can be understood and in order that they be proclaimed and applied and implemented in one's life. Without the Holy Spirit, the Bible is a dead letter, in the same way that justification without the Spirit and without sanctification remains an empty concept.[33]

Ethics as Sanctification Arising Out of Justification

From the importance of the Holy Spirit, we seamlessly come to what ethics mean to Bucer.[34] This is due to the fact that, for Bucer, it is as unthinkable to have faith without a set of ethics deriving therefrom,[35] as it is to have the working of the Holy Spirit without concrete changes being visible.

This becomes clear in an astonishing way as early as his first writings in reaction to the Heidelberg Disputation (1518). It was then, as a young

---

[32] In part. Johannes Müller. Martin Bucers Hermeneutik. op. cit., pp. 41-46 und Willem van't Spijker. „Die Lehre vom Heiligen Geist bei Bucer and Calvin". op. cit., pp. 84-86.

[33] In part. Walter Holsten. „Christentum und nichtchristliche Religion nach der Auffassung Bucers". pp. 9-72 in: Walter Holsten. Das Evangelium und die Völker: Beiträge zur Geschichte und Theorie der Mission: Goßnersche Mission: Berlin, 1939. pp. 138-139.

[34] The most important works regarding his ethics, in particular his social ethics, are: Andreas Gäumann. Reich Christi und Obrigkeit: Eine Studie zum reformatorischen Denken und Handeln Martin Bucers. Zürcher Beiträge zur Reformationsgeschichte 20. Peter Lang: Bern, 2001; Karl Koch. Studium Pietatis: Martin Bucer als Ethiker. Beiträge zur Geschichte und Lehre der Reformierten Kirche 14. Neukirchener Verlag: Neukirchen, 1962 (unfortunately he understands Bucer, however, as a humanist and student of Erasmus and treats fewer sources than Gäumann); Marijn de Kroon. Studien zu Martin Bucers Obrigkeitsverständnis: Evangelisches Ethos und politisches Engagement. Gütersloher Verlagshaus. Gerd Mohn: Gütersloh, 1984; and from an earlier date: Georg Klingenburg. Das Verhältnis Calvins zu Butzer: untersucht auf Grund der wirtschaftsethischen Bedeutung beider Reformatoren. Carl Georgi dissertation: Bonn, 1912; Wilhem Pauck. Das Reich auf Erden: Utopie und Wirklichkeit: Eine Untersuchung zu Butzers 'De Regno Christi' und zur englischen Staatskirche des 16. Jahrhunderts. Arbeiten zur Kirchengeschichte 10. Walter de Gruyter: Berlin, 1928; Wilhelm Pauck. "Martin Bucer's Conception of a Christian State". Princeton Theological Review 2 (1928): 80-88.

[35] According to Gottfried Hammann. Martin Bucer. op. cit., p. 38 dogmatics is always automatically complemented by ethics.

man, that he got to know Martin Luther and became an adherent of his new teaching.[36] Bucer went into detail regarding Luther's theses:

> "In Bucer's rendering of Luther's 'paradoxes,' as he referred to them, Theses 1 and 25 played an important role. For Bucer, all of the emphasis lay on the first thesis (on the work of the will of God). Regarding Thesis 25, (on justification) Bucer held fast to the idea that Christians' actions of course would not be cast off, if only because by faith alone that they are justified. Luther had indeed also emphasized this and had laid, however, the accent on faith, out of which the works of a Christian followed. An initial difference becomes visible at this point. While Luther's theology was concentrated wholeheartedly upon faith in Christ, which then encompassed everything else, with Bucer the Christian's good works that had to arise out of this faith were particularly important. Bucer accepted everything that Luther had developed about man's sin, his failure with respect to the law, and the impossibility of being acceptable before God. He emphatically brought out the idea that a Christian had to place his faith solely upon Christ and not upon his own deeds and achievements. However, in contrast to Luther, Bucer instantly emphasized a much more broadly conceived understanding of the law. God's law certainly accuses and convicts man. But that is not all. That only applies insofar as this law confronts man as something external and foreign. At the same time, the Christian knows of another, new way of dealing with the law: it has to do with internally subscribing to the law and being moved by the Holy Spirit to live and to act according to the law. Bucer calls this, with recourse to Aristotle, an *entelechie*. This is an active and operative energy in Christians. That this fact is made note of is decisive for Bucer. For this reason he correctly piles up concepts at this point. He speaks of the law of God that the Holy Spirit makes operative in people (*lex spiritus*), and this has to do with the law of God's active grace (*lex gratia*). Generally speaking, it has to do with the fruits of grace (*gratia*) and of faith (*fides*) and with a law that presses towards life (*lex vitae*) and that is as well a law that makes everything new (*nova lex*)."[37]

As early as in his thoughts on the Heidelberg Disputation, one finds in Bucer, in place of the contrast of law and gospel, the contradistinction be-

---

[36] Comp. Martin Greschat. „Die Anfänge der reformatorischen Theologie Martin Bucers". pp. 124-140 in: Martin Greschat, J. F. G. Goeters (ed.). Reformation und Humanismus. Robert Stupperich zum 65. Geburtstag. Lutherverlag: Witten, 1969; Martin Brecht. Martin Luther. Bd. 1. Calwer Verlag: Stuttgart, 1983². pp. 210-211; Martin Greschat. Martin Bucer. op. cit., p. 39.
[37] Ibid. p. 40-41.

tween the dead letter and belief in law and a law that is made real by the Holy Spirit.[38]

In good Lutheran style, Karl Koch[39] makes Erasmus' humanism responsible for Bucer's emphasis on ethics, which he never completely overcame. And yet, what Bucer considered as keeping the law is precisely not a work of man. Rather, it is a work of the Holy Spirit. In my opinion, Bucer most consistently filled the vacuum that Luther left in terms of private and social ethics.

> "Above all, Luther emphasized justification by grace alone and addressed much less the question of what that meant for a Christian's actions. For Bucer, by contrast, the latter was more important. There was an additional problem, and that was the understanding of the law. According to Luther's view, God's will is expressed in the law and in his commands. Man knows this will and recognizes at the same time, however, that he is not in a position to fulfill it. In this respect the law is like a mirror, which shows man his inability. The law is thus likened to an accuser that holds up one's sinful being before one's eyes. Although you as man know what is good, you do not do it! Because this is so, the only thing that can help the accused is the judge's unconditional grace. That, in short, is Luther's doctrine of justification, which was also equally held by Bucer. Bucer the Alsatian added some accents. Inasmuch as God's law does not solely remain theory, and people affirm the law internally and conform to it, it is quasi a vessel of the Holy Spirit, out of which vitality, orientation and courage for decisions flow."[40]

Without the Holy Spirit the Bible is also a dead letter. This is no different than considering that the divine law requires the Spirit for it to be put into practice,[41] or that justification without the Spirit and sanctification remains an empty concept.[42] It is this fact that disposed Walter Holsten to say, "Luther's theology was reshaped in Bucer, and indeed in the direction of 'pietism.'"[43] Whether this is actually a change of emphasis compared to Lu-

---

[38] In part. Willem van't Spijker. „Die Lehre vom Heiligen Geist bei Bucer und Calvin". op. cit., pp. 81-83 and Martin Greschat. „Die Anfänge der reformatorischen Theologie Martin Bucers". op. cit., pp. 131-136: comp. Matthieu Arnold for the period 15 years later. „'Dass niemand ihm selbst, sondern anderen leben soll': Das theologische Programm Martin Bucers von 1523 im Vergleich mit Luther". Theologische Beiträge 32 (2001): 237-248.
[39] Karl Koch. Studium Pietatis. op. cit., pp. 10-15.
[40] Hartmut Joisten. Der Grenzgänger Martin Bucer. op. cit., p. 37.
[41] Siehe Martin Greschat. Martin Bucer. op. cit., p. 248.
[42] In part. Walter Holsten. „Christentum und nichtchristliche Religion nach der Auffassung Bucers". op. cit., pp.138-139.
[43] Ibid., p. 137.

ther[44] is something I doubt. In any case, while placing emphasis equal to Luther on justification, Bucer supplemented teaching on justification with additional biblical input.

In my opinion Willem van't Spijker emphasizes that Bucer, as was the case with all Reformers, held closely to so-called forensic justification.[45] W. Peter Stephens has shown through the use of many pieces of evidence that Bucer, in spite of emphasizing the sanctifying power of the Spirit, did not have an inferior view of justification compared to Luther and Calvin.[46]

Bucer, in contrast to Luther, was able to reject any type of works righteousness and yet see the term "wages" in a completely positive light.[47] This doctrine of so-called 'dual justification' is common to both Bucer and Calvin.[48] Bucer saw effective justification standing alongside basic forensic justification, not a condition for but as a consequence of salvation.[49]

Bucer and the Law

The meaning of God's commands are a part of ethics. Just as Calvin did, Bucer also emphasized the entirety of the Old and New Testaments and the shared identity of the Old and New Covenants.[50] Law and Gospel are not

---

[44] Ibid., p. 138.
[45] Willem van't Spijker. „Martin Bucer, Pietist unter den Reformatoren?" pp. 88-101 in: Jan van den Berg, Jan P. van Dooren (ed.). Pietismus und Reveil. Kerkhistorische Bijdragen 7. E. J. Brill: Leiden, 1978. p. 94; ähnlich Karl Koch. Studium Pietatis: Martin Bucer als Ethiker. op. cit., pp. 45-49 and 43, which, however, incorrectly traces Bucer's santification emphasis back to Erasmus.
[46] W. Peter Stephens. The Holy Spirit in the Theology of Martin Bucer. op. cit., pp. 48-70.
[47] Siehe Karl Koch. Studium Pietatis. op. cit., pp. 102-105.
[48] Wilhelm H. Neuser. „Calvins Urteil über den Rechtfertigunggsartikel des Regensburger Buches". pp. 176-194 in: Martin Greschat, J. F. G. Goeters (ed.). Reformation und Humanismus. Robert Stupperich zum 65. Geburtstag. Lutherverlag: Witten, 1969.
[49] In part. Wilhelm Heinrich Neuser . „Bucers Bedeutung für Kirche und Theologie heute". pp. 67-83 in: Frits van der Pol (ed.). Bucer en de kerk. De Groot: Kampen, 1992. pp. 73-74.
[50] In part. Johannes Müller. Martin Bucers Hermeneutik. Quellen und Forschungen zur Reformationsgeschichte 32. Mohn: Gütersloh, 1965. pp. 200-226; Willem van't Spijker. „De eenheid van Oud en Nieuw Verbond bij Martin Bucer". pp. 47-61 in: Willem Balke (ed.). Wegen en gestalten in het gereformeerde protestantisme: een bundel studies over de geschiedenis van het gereformeerde protestantisme aangeboden aan Prof. S. van der Linde. Bolland: Amsterdam, 1976 and Mechthild Köhn. Martin Bucers Entwurf einer Reformation des Erzstiftes Köln: Untersuchung der Entstehungsgeschichte und der Theologie des 'Einfältigen Bedenckens'

allotted to the Old and the New Testaments or to particular parts of the Bible. Rather, both confront us throughout the entirety of the Scriptures.[51]

The Old Testament moral law continues to be the norm for the Christian life,[52] even if it is the Holy Spirit and not the law that changes us. For Bucer, the decisive antithesis is not between works and faith, but rather between works without faith and works with faith.[53] Christ took nothing away from the eternally valid moral law. Rather, he showed us its true meaning.[54]

Admittedly the Law of God can proclaim and judge, but it cannot effect salvation or take away sin.[55] Only grace and promise alone can do this, in the Old as well as the New Testament.

Bucer broke down redemptive history into three eras, above all in their relationship to the law.[56] The Old Testament period is childhood (Latin *puerilis*, *puertia*). The period of the New Testament is the time of growing up into adulthood (*adultior* or *media aetas*). The time beginning with the judgment is the period of full adulthood (*plene virilis aetas*).

For Bucer one finds that love, as Jesus and Paul taught it, is also the essence and the goal of the law.[57] His entire ethic is an ethic of love, and it comes from this source.

Learning from the Anabaptists

Bucer was the only one among the great Reformers who wanted to understand the Anabaptists at all.[58] He sought dialogue with them, and for start-

---

von 1543. Untersuchungen zur Kirchengeschichte 2. Luther-Verlag: Witten, 1966. pp. 83-84.
[51] Also in Walter Holsten. „Christentum und nichtchristliche Religion nach der Auffassung Bucers". op. cit., pp. 105-141, part. pp. 129-131; Walter Holsten. „Christentum und nichtchristliche Religion nach der Auffassung Bucers". op. cit., p. 116 and Karl Koch. Studium Pietatis: Martin Bucer als Ethiker. op. cit., pp. 24-25 and 30-32.
[52] In part. Walter Holsten. „Christentum und nichtchristliche Religion nach der Auffassung Bucers". op. cit., pp. 114-115.
[53] Ibid., p. 116.
[54] H. J. Selderhuis. „Die hermeneutisch-theologische Grundlage der Auffassungen Bucers zur Ehescheidung". op. cit., pp. 233.
[55] Karl Koch. Studium Pietatis. op. cit., p. 67.
[56] Vgl. die Belege bei Andreas Gäumann. Reich Christi und Obrigkeit op. cit., p. 145 und Willem van't Spijker. „Die Lehre vom Heiligen Geist bei Bucer und Calvin". op. cit., p. 83.
[57] See the supporting documents in Karl Koch. Studium Pietatis: Martin Bucer als Ethiker. op. cit., pp. 70-73

ers took the critique of the Anabaptists regarding the condition of the state churches as justified.[59] This even applies to his writings against them, especially his writing against Hans Geneck, a "Faithful Warning" (1528).[60]

> "Bucer's "Faithful Warning" illustrates how closely he stood in many respects to the spiritualistic Anabaptists, beginning with his emphasis on the Holy Spirit and the election of believers by God all the way up to relativizing the sacraments and the esteem shown toward church discipline. But Bucer's borders in relation to the Anabaptists were drawn where he saw them level out Jesus' work of salvation in favor of Jesus' role as an ethical role model, which mankind is called to pursue; he found additional borders when the Anabaptists self-righteously separated themselves from the rest of the church community, and finally, when they refused to take on political responsibility. Precisely this was also the point at which the rulers in Strasbourg became sensitive and took steps against the Anabaptists."[61]

As early as the end of 1526, the first public disputations, together with Capito, began with the best known Anabaptists. In November this occurred with Hans Denck, in December with Michael Sattler. While Bucer and Capito emphasized that love towards one's neighbor should take the shape of responsibility for the common welfare, the Anabaptists placed all weight on the instructions in the Sermon on the Mount.

In December there followed a disputation between Bucer and the Anabaptist Pilgram Marpeck. Bucer's primary objection against him was that the Baptists had veered away from true love that seeks the good of the society. Still

> "Bucer was not untouched by the piety and moral seriousness of this leader of the Anabaptists and his community. All the more imploringly he de-

---

[58] Comp. to Bucer's relationship with the Baptist John S. Oyer. "Bucer and the Anabaptists". pp. 595-602 in: Christian Krieger, Marc Lienhard (ed.). Martin Bucer and Sixteenth Century Europe. Bd. 2. Studies in Medieval and Reformation Thought 53. Brill: Leiden, 1993; Amy Nelson Burnett. "Martin Bucer and the Anabaptist Conflict of Evangelical Confirmation". Mennonite Quarterly Review 68 (1994): 95-122; Stephen E. Buckwalter. „Die Stellung der Straßburger Reformatoren zu den Täufern". Mennonitische Geschichtsblätter 52 (1995): 52-84.

[59] Bucer even maintained relationships with Baptists who lived far away, for instance in the Netherlands. See Willem F. Dankbaar. Martin Bucers Beziehungen zu den Niederlanden. Kerkhistorische Studien 9. Nijhoff: Den Haag, 1961. pp. 15-19.

[60] Martin Bucer. Schriften der Jahre 1524-1528. published by Robert Stupperich. Martini Buceri Opera Omnia, Series I: Deutsche Schriften. vol. 2. Gütersloher Verlagshaus: Gütersloh & Presses Universitaires de France: Paris, 1962. pp. 225-258.

[61] Martin Greschat. Martin Bucer. op. cit., p. 82.

nounced their separation. How much can be accomplished, also with respect to church discipline, when one works together instead of working against each other!"[62]

In August 1538 Bucer gave Philipp of Hessen his word that he would come to Hessen in order to solve the baptismal question. In October of the same year he traveled to Hessen and had discussions with the Anabaptists in Marburg. In November some Anabaptists promised to return to the church if church discipline were to be applied, if other improvements in the church would be made, and if a delay became possible in the time when Anabaptists' children were baptized. The results were the Ziegenhainer Order of Discipline and the Kassel Church Order, both from 1539.[63] In Hessen Bucer achieved a far reaching integration of Anabaptists into the church.[64]

> "Bucer achieved the big breakthrough on November 2 in an extensive discussion with Peter Tesch, who was a leader of the Anabaptists, well-known and respected beyond far beyond Hessen. Tesch was prepared to return to the church with his followers if church discipline were truly to be exercised and his people were to be afforded a slow rapprochement with their pastor and church community. Since he was authorized by the landgrave, Bucer was able to agree. In fact, in his Ziegenhainer Order of Discipline Bucer formulated his well-known ideal of the vibrant, independent church community. Church discipline was a part of this. But just as necessary were Christians who took on responsibility, that is to say, elders. It was also necessary to accompany and educate everyone, especially youth. For this reason Bucer also introduced confirmation.[65] He knew all too well that education and discipline could only become a reality where there were convinced Christians and vibrant church communities. But would not an officially sanctioned church administered by public officials prevent that very thing?"[66]

Samuel Leuenberger was of the opinion that Bucer understood the Anabaptists and could appreciate them, since he did not consider the baptism of

---

[62] Ibid., p. 131.
[63] The text of the so-called Ziegenhainer Zuchtordnung is found in Martin Bucer. Schriften der Jahre 1538-1539. Martin Bucers Deutsche Schriften. vol. 7. Published by Robert Stupperich. Gütersloher Verlagshaus: Gütersloh; Presses Universitaires de France: Paris, 1964. pp. 247-277.
[64] See in this regard in part. Amy Nelson Burnett. "Martin Bucer and the Anabaptist Conflict of Evangelical Confirmation". op. cit., pp. 113-115.
[65] Comp. Gerrit Jan van de Poll. Martin Bucer's Liturgical Ideas. Diss. Groningen, 1957. pp. 48-52.
[66] Martin Greschat. Martin Bucer. op. cit., p. 165; also comp. Andreas Gäumann. Reich Christi und Obrigkeit. op. cit., pp. 504-511.

children a command[67] and for that reason held that delaying the baptism of children was a possibility.[68] In the *censura* (evaluation) of the Anglican liturgy he successfully criticized the echoes of spiritual rebirth in baptism, seeing to it that in the liturgy it was also recognized that children had to later believe for themselves.[69]

> "Even if the Strasbourg Reformer differed in decisive points from the Anabaptists, he had significant points of contact with them: He emphasized, as they did, the meaning of the Holy Spirit, the election of believers, and church discipline."[70]

Bucer was honest enough to see that the Anabaptists were often endearing, that their biblical arguments were worth considering, and that their criticism of the national church was often justified.[71]

For this reason, Bucer achieved something with the Anabaptists that the other Reformers had not achieved. This is due to the fact that he had spoken with them and had taken their concerns about the church's moral laxity seriously.[72] He was friendly to them and esteemed the action of the Holy Spirit in them, which was important to him as well as to them.[73] It is nonsense to think that Bucer only introduced church discipline, confirmation, and other things to harm them.[74]

John S. Oyer has assembled the commonalities (and differences) between Bucer and the Anabaptists in a most clearly arranged way:[75] 1. The sacraments do not convey salvation, and for that reason delaying baptism is possible, 2. The New Testament places a high moral demand on Christians, for which reason church discipline becomes indispensable, 3. We can only be changed by the Holy Spirit, and the Holy Spirit is of indispensable importance for the life of faith as well as for pastoral care and the church community.

---

[67] For comp. to Bucer's theology of baptism see Gottfried Hammann. Martin Bucer. op. cit., pp. 165-175 and W. Peter Stephens. The Holy Spirit in the Theology of Martin Bucer. op. cit., pp. 221-237.
[68] Samuel Leuenberger. Cultus Ancilla Scripturae: Das Book of Common Prayer als erweckliche Liturgie – ein Vermächtnis des Puritanismus. Theologische Dissertationen XVII. Friedrich Reinhardt Verlag: Basel, 1986. p. 53.
[69] Comp. ibid., pp. 37-39.
[70] Hartmut Joisten. Der Grenzgänger Martin Bucer. op. cit., p. 80.
[71] Compilation according to Heinrich Bornkamm. Martin Bucers Bedeutung. op. cit., pp. 14-15.
[72] Also John S. Oyer. "Bucer and the Anabaptists". op. cit., p. 608.
[73] Also ibid., p. 610.
[74] Also ibid., p. 612 and 606 with examples of this view.
[75] John S. Oyer. "Bucer and the Anabaptists". op. cit., in part. pp. 606-607.

Admittedly the positive picture would remain incomplete were it not to be mentioned that Bucer, while he did not have any Anabaptists executed, did indeed increasingly advocate their banishment. At first Bucer, along with Capito, was very conciliatory in practical and political interaction with them. Stephen E. Buckwalter has shown very nicely that 'Strasbourg theology' was a significant reason for the fact that baptism was not fundamentally held to effect salvation and be a source of division of belief.[76] Bucer wrote in 1524 in his Reformation document "Reason and Cause...": "therefore Baptism must be seen as an external thing, freely left, such that God cannot be viewed as bound from any particular time" („so mustu den tauff als ein eusserlich ding frey lassen, das gott ab kein zeit gebunden hat").[77]

While Capito, however, continued to oppose any coercion of the Anabaptists and moved in their direction, Bucer became keener in his argumentation and urged the rather permissive magistrate to drive the Anabaptists out of Strasbourg.[78]

Bucer, however, likewise took the time to not only dispute publicly with the Anabaptists, but rather to thoroughly rebut their teachings on the basis of knowledge he gained in such disputes and in exhaustive study of their writings relating to baptism. In particular, he tried to show from the Holy Scriptures that both taking an oath and a just defensive war were admissible. Likewise he tried to demonstrate that the state was not necessarily wicked and that Christian authorities are possible. Furthermore, he argued in a detailed manner against the Anabaptist Hans Denck with respect to his teaching on free will and universal salvation.

Confirmation

Bucer is the founder of Evangelical confirmation.[79] As early as 1530, he advocated it in Strasbourg without being able to finally push it through.[80] However, in the Ziegenhainer Order of Discipline (1538/39) he gave confirmation its first shape and introduced it in Hessen. The point of confirmation was for children to conclude their Christian instruction by confirming

---

[76] Stephen E. Buckwalter. „Die Stellung der Straßburger Reformatoren zu den Täufern". Mennonitische Geschichtsblätter 52 (1995): 52-84.
[77] Quoted according to ibid., p. 53.
[78] In part. ibid and Andreas Gäumann. Reich Christi und Obrigkeit. op. cit., pp. 326-357.
[79] Comp. in part. Gottfried Hammann. Martin Bucer. op. cit., pp. 242-246; Gerrit Jan van de Poll. Martin Bucer's Liturgical Ideas. Diss. Groningen, 1957. pp. 48-52.
[80] Also Heinrich Bornkamm. Martin Bucers Bedeutung. op. cit., p. 15.

their membership in the church community based on their own confession. Confirmation was the precondition for participating in the Lord's Supper.

Bucer understood confirmation as a renewal of the baptismal confession, just as it is rather substantially understood as a way of taking up the concerns of Anabaptists.[81] This is particularly clear in the Ziegenhainer Order of Discipline. Landgrave Philipp of Hessen had called Bucer to Hessen in 1538 in order to contain the influence of the Anabaptist movement which Bucer did successfully by introducing church discipline and confirmation.

Prior to that time, Erasmus had briefly mentioned confirmation as a pedagogical institution and substitute for communion. Luther had recommended it shortly as a blessing by the church community, but Bucer lifted it to the level of a program and to practical maturity. Confirmation was understood[82] as a personal adoption of the faith and as the integration of youth into the church community.

Confirmation later came to be established in practically all Lutheran and Reformed churches. The Anglican Church also took on confirmation as Bucer had developed it. Indeed, this was due to the fact that Archbishop Cranmer had taken documents for the reformation in Cologne as a model.[83] These documents included a clear regime of confirmation.[84]

In spite of holding to infant baptism, Bucer still wanted to allow for the Anabaptists' idea that as children grow they should, at some point, make the family's faith their own and become mature Christians.[85] As a consequence, confirmation is a bridge between the thinking of the national Protestant church and free Evangelical churches. It is not an accident that almost all free Evangelical churches have introduced something equivalent to confirmation (e.g., completion of Biblical studies).

---

[81] Also in part. Amy Nelson Burnett. "Martin Bucer and the Anabaptist Conflict of Evangelical Confirmation". op. cit., p., Gerrit Jan van de Poll. Martin Bucer's Liturgical Ideas. op. cit., pp. 48-52 and Heinrich Bornkamm. Martin Bucers Bedeutung. op. cit., p. 14.

[82] Also Heinrich Bornkamm. „Martin Bucer: Der dritte deutsche Reformator" (1952). pp. 88-112 in: ders. Das Jahrhundert der Reformation. Vandenhoeck & Ruprecht: Göttingen, 1961. p. 95.

[83] This is generally known. See Samuel Leuenberger. Cultus Ancilla Scripturae. op. cit., pp. 4-5; Hastings Eells. Martin Bucer. op. cit., p. 411.

[84] Mechthild Köhn. Martin Bucers Entwurf einer Reformation des Erzstiftes Köln. op. cit., pp. 137-141.

[85] Comp. Gerrit Jan van de Poll. Martin Bucer's Liturgical Ideas. op. cit., pp. 48-52.

Pastoral Care as a Sign of Jesus' Church

The most important statements regarding church[86] order that were influenced by Bucer include Strasbourg (1534), Ziegenhain and Kassel (1539), and Cologne (1543, composed with Melanchthon), the latter playing a weighty role in the *Book of Common Prayer*. There are common elements in all of them that were meant to ensure that faith was seen as a personal possession that influences daily life, for instance in confirmation, pastoral care, and church discipline.

In the area of Reformed theology, there are a number of documents which arose that were intended to do nothing less than programmatically implement an understanding of pastoral care of the individual and the church community. Precursors were Zwingli's "The Shepherd" (*Der Hirt*, 1524), and surely as a high point Bucer's own document "On true Pastoral Care"[87] (*Von der wahren Seelsorge*, 1538), which presented a very sophisticated program of church education. This represents the very first Evangelical pastoral theology.[88]

---

[86] The two most comprehensive accounts of Bucer's ecclesiology are: Gottfried Hammann. Martin Bucer: 1491-1551. Zwischen Volkskirche und Bekenntnisgemeinschaft. Veröffentlichungen des Instituts für Europäische Geschichte 139. Steiner: Stuttgart, 1989 (French original Entre la secte e la cite, 1984); Willem van't Spijker. The Ecclesiastical Office in the Thought of Martin Bucer. Studies in Medieval and Reformation Thought 57. Brill: Leiden, 1996 (Dutch De ambten bij Martin Bucer. Diss. Amsterdam, 1970); comp. additionally the collected anthology David F. Wright (ed.). Martin Bucer: Reforming Church and Society. Cambridge University Press: Cambridge, 1994.

[87] Martin Bucer. Von der wahren Seelsorge und dem rechten hirten Dienst ... Rihel: Straßburg, 1538 (original in many German libraries); reproduced in Martin Bucer. Schriften der Jahre 1538-1539. Martin Bucers Deutsche Schriften. vol. 7. Published by von Robert Stupperich. Gütersloher Verlagshaus: Gütersloh; Presses Universitaires de France: Paris,1964. pp. 67-245.

[88] Comp. above all Bucer's pastoral concept: Reinhold Friedrich. „Martin Bucer". pp. 85-101 in: Christian Möller (ed.). Geschichte der Seelsorge in Einzelporträts. vol. 2. Von Martin Luther bis Matthias Claudius. Vandenhoeck & Ruprecht: Göttingen, 1995; Gottfried Hammann. „Martin Bucer: Sa vision de l'Église selon le traité 'Von der waren Seelsorge' et développement de la discipline ecclésiastique à Strasbourg de 1524 à 1549. pp. 73-89 in: Marc Lienhard (ed.). Croyants et Sceptiques au XVIe siècle: Le dossier des 'Epicuriens'. Recherches et Documents 30. Libr. Istra: Strasbourg, 1981; Gerhard Müller. „Seelsorge und Kirchenzucht. Martin Bucers Vorstellungen von Kirchenleitung". 143-155 in: Rudolf Landau, Günter R. Schmidt (ed.). 'Daß allen Menschen geholfen werde ...': Theologische und anthropologische Beiträge für Manfred Seitz zum 65. Geburtstag. Calwer Verlag: Stuttgart, 1993.

> "For the first time, in Bucer's document 'On true Pastoral Care,' one finds a theological and Biblically based theory of pastoral care. It is a systematic and complete overview. Bucer establishes his argumentation on Holy Scripture, supports his argumentation historically, and explains with enthusiasm the necessity he sees in conducting pastoral care as one of the required signs of the Reformation. He views this as a continual process of 'improvement' and not as a one-time historical event."[89]

Pastoral care is thereby deeply rooted in Bucer's understanding of the foundational elements of the Christian faith.

> "In his teaching of pastoral care and shepherding, Bucer sees a relationship between Christology and ecclesiology. He emphasized that Christ is the one who calls people to be pastorally cared for and exercises pastoral care through these same people. Pastoral care is simultaneously the work of Christ and the church in its entirety. Care for people is the intrinsic task of the church."[90]

Christians should be led away from sin and guided to everything good. Bucer's pastoral care encompasses the bodily and spiritual domains and is molded by ethics, church education, and church discipline. In any case, Bucer assumed, contrary to Luther, that in the Bible he could find the will of God for the concrete, everyday life of the Christian and of the church. He also assumed that in the Bible he could find the way to pastorally ascertain this will of God. The influences coming from the Anabaptists, as well as the contention he had with them, can be sensed everywhere. In 1543 the Bohemian Brethren had the work printed in Czech.

Bucer's understanding of pastoral care is not only pastoral psychology, but also the 'communities', that have been discussed before, had the task of encouraging everyone to exercise pastoral care. Every member of the church should exercise pastoral care in the way the Good Shepherd did as a paragon for everyone.[91]

> "In Bucer's understanding of pastoral care there are various focal points in which respective strengths and weaknesses are recognizable.
> 1. Pastoral care is the responsibility of all Christians. There is no point in the first decades of the Reformation where the axiom of the 'royal priesthood' of all believers is taken as seriously as in Bucer's writing entitled "On True Pastoral Care." The conscious emphasis on the responsibility of all Christians to exercise pastoral care is as contemporary an issue as ever.

---

[89] Reinhold Friedrich. „Martin Bucer". op. cit., p. 98.
[90] Ibid., p. 98.
[91] See the supporting documents in Karl Koch. Studium Pietatis. op. cit., p. 56-58.

The inclusion of civil authorities into the exercise of pastoral care in his day was surely to be viewed critically.

2. In exemplary manner, on the basis of practical relationships Bucer associates his teaching on offices with the 'priesthood of all believers,' but he does not place offices over the latter. Calvin put Bucer's teaching on offices into practice in Geneva using somewhat different concepts.

3. A significant importance is assigned to Bucer's thinking about the relationship between pastoral care and the church."[92]

In any case, pastoral care stands in the service of love within the church and exemplifies Christian unity.

> "True pastoral care has an ecumenical meaning: Through personal conversation it should help overcome splits within Christianity, and it should do so by bringing those back to the church who err, who stand at a distance, or who are unbelievers."[93]

It is not by accident that one finds the following as the subheading of his writing on pastoral care:

> "You will find within these pages the essential means by which we can move from miserable and pernicious religious splits and divisions to true unity within the church and for the sake of the same good Christian order. This is not only for the community of believers, but it is also useful for pastors and overseers."[94]

Church Discipline

Everything that we have heard up until now about the importance of the Holy Spirit, of ethics, and about community come together to be part of Bucer's signature feature, church discipline.[95] For Bucer a church without

---

[92] Reinhold Friedrich. „Martin Bucer". op. cit., pp. 98-99; comp. the points 3.-5. pp. 99-100 with justified criticism of Bucer, for instance, that he mentions no special pastoral care for the sick, the suffering, the challenged, or the heavy-hearted.

[93] Reinhold Friedrich. „Martin Bucer". op. cit., p. 98

[94] Quoted according to ibid., p. 91.

[95] The most comprehensive study on Bucer's church discipline is: Amy N. Burnett. The Yoke of Christ: Martin Bucer and Christian Discipline. Sixteenth Century Essays and Studies 26. Sixteenth Century Journal Publ.: Kirksville (MO), 1994; comp. Ann Nelson Burnett. "Church Discipline and Moral Reformation in the Thought of Martin Bucer". Sixteenth Century Journal 22 (1991): 439-456. See additionally Gottfried Hammann. Martin Bucer: 1491-1551. Zwischen Volkskirche und Bekenntnisgemeinschaft. op. cit., p. 70-71 and 191-206; Mechthild Köhn.

church discipline is in itself a contradiction and therefore unthinkable.[96] At the same time one has to admittedly emphasize that Bucer understood church discipline from the standpoint of pastoral care and viewed exclusion only as a last resort.[97] What was involved was the continual pastoral care of Christians.[98] Martin Greschat tellingly summarized what moved Bucer at this point.

> "On the one hand he wanted to elevate to consciousness – and he therefore emphasized it again and again – that in the church community of believing Christians the Holy Spirit is at work. For that reason there had to be vital and active Christians who were prepared to take responsibility for their fellow men as well as for the church in general. In his picture of the church as a community of believing Christians created by the Holy Spirit, there had to not only be a vital diversity and organizational joint responsibility. There was also first and foremost the need for an earnest will to exercise church discipline. For Bucer, hesitation or reservation at this point meant logical indecisiveness in the central question of faith and trust with respect to Christ. 'We have to decide once and for all whether we truly have the will to be Christians.'"[99]

As far as Bucer is concerned, this has to do with nothing less than bringing belief and life into harmony, whereby church discipline, as an element of pastoral care, should make a significant contribution.

> "Bucer viewed the Strasbourg church's 'most weighty deficiency and error' to be the fact that for them belief and life clearly diverged and – if at all – church discipline was no more than halfheartedly taken seriously."[100]

Martin Bucers Entwurf einer Reformation des Erzstiftes Köln. op. cit., p. 142-146 (on Köln); Hartmut Joisten. Der Grenzgänger Martin Bucer. op. cit., pp. 115-118 (on Hessen).

[96] Also Paul D. L. Avis. "The True Church' in Reformation Theology". Scottish Journal of Theology 30 (1977): 319-345, here p. 336, on the basis of the document 'Von der waren Seelsorge' (1538).

[97] See especially the most thorough investigation on the topic, Amy N. Burnett. The Yoke of Christ. op. cit., in part. p. 221.

[98] In part. Gottfried Hammann. „Die ekklesiologischen Hintergründe zur Bildung von Bucers 'Christlichen Gemeinschaften' in Straßburg (1546-1548)". Zeitschrift für Kirchengeschichte 105 (1994): 344-360, here p. 292 and Amy N. Burnett. The Yoke of Christ. op. cit.. and Ann Nelson Burnett. "Church Discipline and Moral Reformation in the Thought of Martin Bucer". op. cit.

[99] Martin Greschat. Martin Bucer. op. cit., p. 160.

[100] Hartmut Joisten. Der Grenzgänger Martin Bucer. op. cit., p. 141.

An important differentiation is, however, to be made here, because Bucer was vehemently in favor of pastoral care and church discipline, but albeit not in favor of a community of those who were ethically complete or perfected. Even while Bucer emphasized the importance of the Holy Spirit, he still differentiated himself from the so-called 'spiritualists' of his time, in that he saw an important place in the church community for the weak and imperfect[101] not only a place for the perfected.

Lay Elders

From church discipline we move organically to one of Bucer's weightiest 'discoveries,' the lay elder. In October 1531 church elders, who were responsible for church discipline and correct doctrine, were installed in Strasbourg. Each parish was to have 3 wardens. Bucer put the wardens on the same level as the elders in the New Testament. The new concept of lay elders was adopted from Calvin and played a large role in the Reformed theology and practice. It became universally important and leaped across to many other Protestant churches, so that today it is largely a part of standard Protestantism.

Even though he clearly desired it for lay elders, due to an inadequate separation of church and state, a situation for which Bucer was not completely without guilt, his concept came to naught in Strasbourg.

> "For many years Bucer believed that wardens could be changed from the non-Christian model to an ecclesiastical church-prescribed role. However, he soon realized that he was mistaken to think that he could reshape a position which had begun by order of the authorities into an organ of pure church discipline. According to the intentions of the council, the office of church warden remained 'a civil honorary office, appointed and authorized by a magistrate.'"[102]

It can be added at this point that Bucer did not back up the teaching of the four offices that Calvin taught.[103] Bucer had a more flexible understanding of the number and types of offices, which are dependent on the situation. With Bucer, new offices are conceivable over time.[104] The basic functions

---

[101] In part. Karl Koch. Studium Pietatis. op. cit., p. 53 with supporting documents.
[102] Reinhold Friedrich. „Martin Bucer". op. cit., p. 89.
[103] Part. clear in Gottfried Hammann. Martin Bucer. op. cit., pp. 58-59 and 226-227; comp. on the whole to Bucer's teaching on offices ibid., pp. 208-250.
[104] Ibid., pp. 224-226.

of all the offices are *docere* (to teach), *monere* (to exhort), and *diligere* (to serve).[105]

Although a precursor of the exegetical views of Calvin, Martin Bucer was also principally in favor of bishops, particularly in cases where the bishops themselves, as in England, advanced the Reformation.[106] However, he fundamentally rejected their sacramental position and the fact that they had a legal right to require obedience. This was the only way that he held it was possible in the Cologne Reformation and in England for the Reformed church to maintain its old structure of Bishops.[107] One should, however, bear in mind that actually Bucer was talking about the pastor of a church community when he used the term bishop, as Gottfried Hammann has fittingly shown.[108] Reinhold Friedrich writes in this connection:

> "According to our present day designations, he differentiated between bishops, church pastors, preachers, church elders and church deacons. In the process it did not have to do with four offices in actual fact. Rather, according to Bucer's view (on the basis of 1 Timothy 3 and in accepted agreement with the original church) there were only two offices, those of elder and deacon. With respect to the former office, those are included who are considered servants in the word (bishops, pastors, preachers, elders): they served in the word, in doctrine, in the administration of the sacraments and in church discipline. The second office (deacon) consists in the care for the poor and in social duties, meaning the works of the diaconate."[109]

Christian Communities

After decades of work with the Reformation in Strasbourg, Bucer became increasingly pessimistic about reforming the entire society and the entire church. In Strasbourg he experienced no cooperation between the church and authorities commensurate with the Gospel.

> "In order to remedy things, he proposed starting Christian communities that were consciously and without reservation wanting to be serious about the demands of the Gospel. In such communities there was to be a higher level of commitment and visible fidelity to the message of the Bible. People were

---

[105] According to ibid., pp. 58-59.
[106] Gerrit Jan van de Poll. Martin Bucer's Liturgical Ideas. Diss. Groningen, 1957. p. 69.
[107] See, e.g., Mechthild Köhn. Martin Bucers Entwurf einer Reformation des Erzstiftes Köln. op. cit., p. 163-164.
[108] Gottfried Hammann. Martin Bucer. op. cit., pp. 235-237.
[109] Reinhold Friedrich. „Martin Bucer". op. cit., p. 93.

to voluntarily submit to church discipline based on the Ten Commandments. That such communities existed in St. Thomas and Jung-Sankt-Peter is first mentioned in the minutes of the Strasbourg council for February 21, 1547."[110]

Due to the poor spiritual state of the church in Strasbourg, Bucer increasingly pursued the gathering of active believers and serious Christians into special 'Christian communities,'[111] as he called them, which were a type of core church community organized into house churches. Via Bible study, prayer, pastoral case and simply being there for each other, community life was intended to become practical. These special communities were to foster the growth of the church community from within and function as a role model. Members were to be on their own, separate lists and regularly visited by pastors.

"The model that Bucer developed began as a voluntary union of committed Christians and had as its target the gradual winning over of the city's entire church community. The members of the 'Christian community' were to choose men in each parish who were to counsel, teach, and work together with the pastors and wardens while exercising a supervisory function. Bucer apparently hoped to thereby prevent large communities and small groups from breaking apart. Bucer left no doubt that he now saw this as decisive and therefore as something that should determine and influence everything. Virtually all church-related work, then, had to do with getting people affiliated with these communities as well as consequently achieving a situation where remaining Christians, who did not 'want to commit themselves to right, true obedience to the church' were drawn back in. Bucer saw this problem, but he viewed it as a secondary issue. Above all, warnings about either a new papacy or a situation where the Anabaptists' agenda triumphed in Strasbourg did not convince him. 'We are a long way away from expulsion and banishment. Rather, we solely desire that out of the duty and debt of our ecclesiastical service, all those who wish to be right and true Christians, commit themselves to obedience to the church and thereby witness freely and publicly give witness to what they believe about the Gospel and

---

[110] Hartmut Joisten. Der Grenzgänger Martin Bucer. op. cit., p. 141.
[111] The most important current investigation is Gottfried Hammann. Martin Bucer: 1491-1551. Zwischen Volkskirche und Bekenntnisgemeinschaft. op. cit. in toto, in part. pp. 288-313; also comp. Gottfried Hammann. „Die ekklesiologischen Hintergründe zur Bildung von Bucers 'Christlichen Gemeinschaften' in Straßburg (1546-1548)". Zeitschrift für Kirchengeschichte 105 (1994): 344-360; Amy N. Burnett. The Yoke of Christ: Martin Bucer and Christian Discipline. op. cit., pp. 180-207 and Andreas Gäumann. Reich Christi und Obrigkeit. op. cit., pp. 396-403 and 118-119.

what we, by God's grace, have been preaching to them for such a long period of time.'"[112]

Even if one has to recognize that Bucer failed in Strasbourg with his concept of 'Christian community,' his understanding of church discipline, and confirmation,[113] he is still the only Reformer who thought through such a concept in detail and put it into practice. Luther, for instance, who in the preface to his 'German mass' made the comment that whoever wanted to be a serious Christian should also assemble for worship service, never really got beyond that point.[114] The Bucerian communities largely fell into oblivion in the national churches (with the exception of pietism), because they were sensed to be a foreign substance and an undesired free church incursion in the national church. In 1934 Werner Bellardi was the first person to make reference to Christian communities that arose beginning in 1545.[115]

Of decisive importance is Bucer's non-published document entitled "On the Church's Deficiencies and Error" (*Von der Kirchen mengel und fähl*),[116] dating from around 1547. Bucer wanted to guarantee that worldly authorities were limited to their domain and did not hinder the church in pastoral care and in the building up of the church. Indeed the city council adopted a new order of church discipline in January 1548 but allowed the church no significant freedom with this new ordinance.

---

[112] Martin Greschat. Martin Bucer. op. cit., p. 211.
[113] The history of the dispute between Bucer and the Strasbourg magistrate relating to church discipline is depicted at length by Andreas Gäumann. Reich Christi und Obrigkeit. op. cit., 359-406.
[114] Comp. Werner Bellardi. Die Vorstufen der Collegia Pietatis bei Philipp Jakob Spener. Brunnen: Gießen, 1994. pp. 72-79 and 19-21.
[115] Werner Bellardi. Die Geschichte der 'Christlichen Gemeinschaft' in Straßbourg (1546/1550): Der Versuch einer 'zweiten Reformation'. Quellen und Forschungen zur Reformationsgeschichte 18. Heinsius: Leipzig, 1934; Reprint: Johnson Repr. Corp.: New York, 1971; comp. preliminary work, which was published shortly after his death: 1931 Werner Bellardi. Die Vorstufen der Collegia Pietatis bei Philipp Jakob Spener. Brunnen: Gießen, 1994. pp. 28-71 (Reprint of an unpublished dissertation, Breslau 1930).
[116] Martin Bucer. Die letzten Straßburger Jahre 1546-149: Schriften zur Gemeindereformation und zum Augsburger Interim. Published by Robert Stupperich. Martini Buceri Opera Omnia, Series I: Deutsche Schriften. vol. 17. Gütersloher Verlagshaus: Gütersloh & Presses Universitaires de France: Paris, 1981. Beginning on p. 156. The volume contains Bucer's writings on Christian community, among others.

"With his incessant urgings for independent church discipline, Bucer made himself unpopular among those who governed, an unpopularity which became complete with his participation in the organization of 'Christian communities.'"[117]

The council of the city of Strasbourg generally found that the communities undermined the Christian West.

"Bucer's concept of a people's and confessional church model is addressed, among other things, in his 1547 essay entitled 'On the Church's Deficiencies and Error.' In it he additionally held up a mirror to the city leaders and pointed out to them 'that worldly authorities were limited to their domain and were not to assume a greater grip on things than was enjoined on them and commanded of them by God. This means that worldly authority is ordered to seek to avoid hindering the affairs of the church.' Even though the Strasbourg council passed a bill on church discipline on January 25, 1548 and thereby complied with Reformers' demands, the relationship between the committees and Bucer had already been strongly tarnished in the meantime. City leaders were unable to warm to the inception of Christian communities and the demand for greater church independence. They viewed it as a state that existed within a state and believed that with it a power would unfold that would remove power at their disposal. Additionally, they supposed that these communities would become a source of new sectarianism. As a result, the council demanded the disbandment of the communities. All attempts to convince the city leaders of their importance and relevance failed, particularly because they were also disputed among pastors."[118]

In numerous documents Bucer summarized the objections his opponents had against the communities[119] and refuted them meticulously. The objections sound very modern and have in large part been repeated in later centuries by mainline churches with respect to Puritanism, Pietism and free Evangelical churches.

– "'We do not live in those times and we do not have churches like Jesus Christ and the dear apostles had. Rather, for us it is like the times of the prophets. The apostles had small congregations and more devoted people; we have large and cold congregations, of a type that such communities cannot be established and cared for.'
– 'If such Christian discussion communities as well as former requirements

---

[117] Martin Greschat. Martin Bucer. op. cit., p. 230.
[118] Hartmut Joisten. Der Grenzgänger Martin Bucer. op. cit., p. 143.
[119] Comp. the list of writings and the objections in Gottfried Hammann. Martin Bucer. op. cit., p. 307-308.

(within the ancient church) are to be so highly thought of and so necessary, then why have we not started with this a long time ago? – And how is it that other Evangelical churches have not started such gatherings and communities?"

'One cannot maintain that such a special seeking and gathering of Christians is necessary and that it would bring an improvement (to the church). If we only allowed volunteer participants into such gatherings, it would be the same people who without this would be willing to have pastoral care. Others, in contrast, would not be willing to enter such communities. So you will be only a small group within your community and congregation.

– 'Pious people are still susceptible and misled to feel arrogant and to disparagingly judge others. From this there would develop a separation between citizens.'

– 'Those who would come together would think of themselves as better and judge others prematurely, disdain them, and think more of their special discussion meetings than of general worship times with preaching and the administration of the sacraments. They would regard their fellow humanity in an ungodly manner.'

– "At various times we have written repeatedly to Anabaptist congregations and complained that they were drawing people away from the general times of preaching . . .'

– 'Although these gatherings might look initially as if they were created and practiced in a Christian manner, the danger exists that they can be later abused. If this were to spread, the fear is that it could lead to a reinstatement of excommunication and a change in the authorities.'

Thus many people consider it not necessary to institute (. . .) a special community. Thus so many people shy away from this and fear deleterious results from it. And scores of people thus think that in our time we are not presented with an opportunity for this . . .' – You yourselves do not have half agreement about the thing among yourselves!'"[120]

Against his opposition, Bucer always held vehemently to fidelity to the witness of Scripture.[121]

"The attempt to create Christian communities inspired Bucer's literary fervor. He composed numerous documents in this respect, of which several offered a helpful summary of his understanding of the church. Four of these writings have become especially noteworthy: ... Ecclesiologically speaking, the first work mentioned immediately above, on the basis of its synthesis of

---

[120] From Bucer's 'Die Gegner der kleinen Gemeinschaften' (1547/48), quoted from Gottfried Hammann. Martin Bucer. Gestalten des Protestantismus von gestern und heute. Christliches Verlags-Haus: Stuttgart, 1989.

[121] Comp. Gottfried Hammann. „Die ekklesiologischen Hintergründe zur Bildung von Bucers 'Christlichen Gemeinschaften' ...". op. cit., pp. 352-354.

theoretical and practical statements on the project of community, is the most extensively formulated work. It is difficult, however, to place a specific date on it. In addition to these four documents, there are others that appeared that were valuable for the history of the communities but otherwise only confirm the basic thoughts of these major writings."[122]

Bucer wanted to have a national church for everyone as well as a church of only true believers.[123] This concept foundered, but it remains a warning to us. The warning is that valid concerns of a national church as well as those of a community of confessing Christians both need to be taken into account and not too hastily lost from sight in denominational trench warfare.

Incidentally, the 'Christian communities' were meant to serve the cause of unity. This is due to the fact that Bucer was convinced, primarily on the basis of Ephesians 4, that mature Christians were the precondition for true unity. Moreover, unity and fellowship within the church was something to be practiced in small groups.[124]

The Meaning of the Family in the Church Community

Even if there were some echoes in Luther and more so in Calvin about the idea of the family and their worship being the core of the church, it was only Bucer who seriously discussed the concept in connection with house church communities and who called for the family to be more highly valued in the church.[125]

On this issue as well, Bucer's thinking and actions served as a bridge-building function between the national church on one side and the Anabaptist free church on the other.

---

[122] Gottfried Hammann. Martin Bucer. op. cit., p. 297.
[123] In part. Elsie Anne McKee. Elders and the Plural Ministry: The Role of Exegetical History in Illuminating John Calvin's Theology. Travaux d'Humanisme et Renaissance Librairie 223. Droz: Genf, 1988. p. 19.
[124] Distinguished so in Gottfried Hammann. „Die ekklesiologischen Hintergründe zur Bildung von Bucers 'Christlichen Gemeinschaften' ...". op. cit., pp. 347-349 and 357-358.
[125] Very well compiled in Gottfried Hammann, Martin Bucer. op. cit., pp. 127-133 Gemeinschaft 132-133 and 288-289.

Apologetics and the Priesthood of Believers

It is not surprising that Bucer held that the proclamation of the Gospel was something for every individual believer and for that reason every Christian should be in the position to explain his faith and pass it on.

> "In addition to the unity of the church, since the middle of the 1530's Bucer concerned himself increasingly with the self-image of each Christian and that of the Christian church. Through all the conflicts and challenges of his time it became increasingly clear to Bucer that every Christian must be prepared and in the position to give an account of his or her faith to others. In the things he published, Bucer wanted to provide assistance in this, particularly in his commentaries on books of the Bible. His exegetical magnum opus served chiefly to this end. It was a commentary on the Letter to the Romans dedicated to the Archbishop of Canterbury, Thomas Cranmer."[126]

It is generally the case that as far as Bucer was concerned, good Bible interpretation and Christian maturity were closely related.

> "Each individual Christian has to be in a position to give an account of his or her faith. From very early on, Bucer called emphatically for this along with all Reformers. However, from the beginning Bucer was intent on achieving this basic principle in a practical manner. The fact that year for year Bucer continued with his interpretation of the books of the Bible, not only for theologians but rather for all educated and interested citizens, is the clearest piece of evidence for this."[127]

This is also practically expressed in his commentaries, because Bucer placed a high value on elucidating the historical situation in which respective Biblical statements were made. For his Old Testament interpretation, he expressly consulted medieval Jewish commentaries.

Bucer did not tire of pointing out to his readers that they themselves had to test and judge so that they could come up with their own standpoint. This particularly applied to non-theologians.

In addition to that, religious training as well as one's own theological continuing education was a lifelong requirement for every Christian![128]

---

[126] Hartmut Joisten. Der Grenzgänger Martin Bucer. op. cit., p. 110.
[127] Martin Greschat. Martin Bucer. op. cit., p. 155.
[128] See Andreas Gäumann. Reich Christi und Obrigkeit. op. cit., p. 275.

The Pietist among the Reformers

In 1900 August Lang called Bucer the "Pietist among the Reformers"[129] in a saying that became popular. He went as far as to say that Bucer was the "initiator and father of pietism."[130] There are "urgings of a pietistic nature,"[131] and there are many parallels such as the emphasis on conversion, the difference between these and those believers, sanctification, the Holy Spirit, and concrete community. By 1941 he only found "seeds of Pietism,"[132] by which the Englishmen and Puritan William Perkins achieved the position of the actual father of pietism. "On the other hand, there is indeed a certain sense in which M. Butzer was, in his religious manner, his forerunner."[133]

Since that time there has been an intensive debate as to whether Bucer was a pietist or not. Johannes Wallmann[134] and Willem Spijker,[135] for example, basically reject this idea. Werner Neuser, on the other hand, agrees with Land and points out that Philipp Jakob Spener, the 'official' father of German pietism, had Bucer's report "On the Church's Deficiencies and Error," "reprinted for the defense of his 'collegia pietatis.'"[136]

---

[129] See August Lang. Der Evangelienkommentar Martin Butzers und die Grundzüge seiner Theologie. Studien zur Geschichte der Theologie und der Kirche 2,2. Dieterich: Leipzig, 1900; Reprint Scientia: Aalen, 1972. pp. 8 and 373; comp. pp. 137 and 374.
[130] Ibid., p. 137; comp. pp. 374 and 364.
[131] August Lang. Puritanismus und Pietismus. op. cit., p. 13.
[132] Ibid., p. 130.
[133] Ibid.
[134] Johannes Wallmann. „Bucer und der Pietismus". pp. 715-732 in: Christian Krieger, Marc Lienhard (ed.). Martin Bucer and Sixteenth Century Europe. vol. 2. Studies in Medieval and Reformation Thought 53. Brill: Leiden, 1993.
[135] Willem van't Spijker. „Martin Bucer, Pietist unter den Reformatoren?". pp. 88-101 in: Jan van den Berg, Jan P. van Dooren (ed.). Pietismus und Reveil. Kerkhistorische Bijdragen 7. E. J. Brill: Leiden, 1978, in part. pp. 88-89 and 99-101.
[136] Werner Neuser. „Von Zwingli und Calvin bis zur Synode von Westminster". op. cit., pp. 223-224; comp. Johannes Wallmann. Philipp Jakob Spener und die Anfänge des Pietismus. Beiträge zur historischen Theologie 42. Tübingen, 1986². pp. 32 and 270. Comp. Werner Bellardi. Die Vorstufen der Collegia Pietatis bei Philipp Jakob Spener. pp. 28-29 for the details of the history of reprints of Bucer's document by Spener see 'Vertheidigung der so genandten Collegiourum pietatis Hiebevor von Martino Bucero dem berühmten Theologo' (Copy of the original is in the University of Gießen library).

"From Calvin's church up to the communities of pietism, the broad basis of his ecclesiology served as a support for the most varied types of church communities."[137]

I think that this debate can be easily resolved. It can be shown that Bucer is neither the father of pietism nor were the fathers of pietism directly influenced by him or his writings. Whoever dismisses the designation of 'pietist among the Reformers' as only an anachronism[138] overlooks the many parallels between pietism, Puritanism, and Bucer. Bucer was in many respects a forerunner of pietism, for which reason he is referred to even if one only heard about him much later. Accordingly, Gottfried Hammann correctly shows that 130 years later Spener was not influenced by Bucer. And yet, at the same time, he was not just incidentally glad to hear about Bucer's writings and have them reprinted.[139] After all, Wallmann also has to confess: "Only in the Moravian Church did one refer to Bucer."[140]

Wilhelm Heinrich Neuser, by the way, pointed out that pietism does not only have a forerunner in Bucer insofar as one deals with the idea of a 'church within a church,' but rather in overcoming confessional boundaries as well.[141]

The Lutheran Walter Holsten viewed Bucer's pietistic accent very critically: "Luther's theology experienced a reshuffling in Bucer, and indeed it was one in the direction of 'pietism.'"[142] "Pietas" was therefore an important concept for Bucer.[143] There is a shifting of the accent from justification to sanctification, from word to the Spirit, and from the church to

---

[137] Gottfried Hammann. Martin Bucer. op. cit., p. 76.
[138] For instance Willem van't Spijker. „Martin Bucer, Pietist unter den Reformatoren?". op. cit., p. 100.
[139] Comp. to Bucer's 'Gemeinschaften' as a precursor of Spener's assemblage in Werner Bellardi. Die Vorstufen der Collegia Pietatis bei Philipp Jakob Spener. op. cit., pp. 28-71.
[140] Johannes Wallmann. „Bucer und der Pietismus". op. cit., p. 731.
[141] Wilhelm Heinrich Neuser. „Bucers Bedeutung für Kirche und Theologie heute". pp. 67-83 in: Frits van der Pol (ed.). Bucer en de kerk. De Groot: Kampen, 1992. pp. 77-79.
[142] Walter Holsten. „Christentum und nichtchristliche Religion nach der Auffassung Bucers". pp. 9-72 in: Walter Holsten. Das Evangelium und die Völker: Beiträge zur Geschichte und Theorie der Mission: Goßnersche Mission: Berlin, 1939. p. 137.
[143] The best investigation regarding this concept Bucer uses is Willem van't Spijker. „Martin Bucer, Pietist unter den Reformatoren?". op. cit., pp. 90-99.

community.[144] We have addressed this topic within the framework of the question of justification.

Willem van't Spijker has pointed out that in contrast to Bucer, within pietism what is missing is the idea of theocracy, that is to say, the teaching that all spheres of life are to be brought into submission to God.[145] The theocratic line of thinking was all the more evidently anchored within 'England's pietists,' the Puritans.

The Puritan among the Reformers

Bucer had an enormous effect on the emergence and development of the Anglican state church,[146] and he helped to shape Anglican liturgy. Samuel Leuenberger speaks about this as the 'revivalist side'[147] in Bucer's teaching and liturgy.

Nevertheless, his true legacy in England is not the Anglicans. Rather, reformed Puritans came into Bucer's inheritance,[148] above all via his ethical magnum opus 'De Regno Christi' (1550). Predestination, moral earnestness, the Sabbath, the emphasis on practical community, the Presbyter-

---

[144] Walter Holsten. „Christentum und nichtchristliche Religion nach der Auffassung Bucers". op. cit., pp. 137-138.

[145] Willem van't Spijker. „Martin Bucer, Pietist unter den Reformatoren?". op. cit., pp. 100-101.

[146] The classics at Bucer's time in England are older: Andrew Edward Harvey. Martin Bucer in England. Bauer: Marburg, 1906; Constantin Hopf. Martin Bucer and the English Reformation. Basil Blackwell: Oxford, 1946; Hastings Eells. Martin Bucer. op. cit., pp. 401-414; N. Scott Amos. "It is Fallow Ground Here: Martin Bucer as Critic of the English Reformation". Westminster Theological Journal 61 (1999): 41-52.

[147] Samuel Leuenberger. Cultus Ancilla Scripturae. op. cit., p. 53 (with additional literature).

[148] Also Heinrich Bornkamm. Martin Bucers Bedeutung. op. cit., pp. 33-34; Wilhelm Pauck. Das Reich auf Erden. op. cit., p. 81 and August Lang. Puritanismus und Pietismus: Studien zu ihrer Entwicklung von M. Butzer bis zum Methodismus. op. cit. 1. Kapitel „Butzer und der Puritanismus". pp. 13-71, in part. pp. 22-38. Jürgen-Burkhard Klautke. Recht auf Widerstand gegen die Obrigkeit? Eine systematisch-theologische Untersuchung zu den Bestreitungs- und Rechtfertigungsbemühungen von Gewaltanwendung gegen die weltliche Macht (bis zum 18. Jahrhundert). 2 Bde. Kok: Kampen (NL), 1995, It is too bad that Klautke, who otherwise very extensively and exhaustively treats the conception of the state held by Reformed theologians, does not devote a separate section to Bucer, apart from a short outline at the end under England (ibid., pp. 519-520). Klautke rightly ascribes the strong inclusion of the Old Testament by Puritans and in Anglo-Saxon theology to Bucer, which would have justified his own account.

ian teaching on offices, and the emphasis on the Holy Spirit are all similarities between Bucer and the Puritans. This becomes clear, for instance, in the fact that Puritans enforced church discipline while Anglican authors such as Richard Hooker rejected it.[149]

In no way should one look at Bucer as a cheap defender of the establishment,[150] especially during his time in England. The Puritan willingness to protest against the king and the archbishop was already set in motion by Bucer.

Bucer wanted Christian Unity

"According to his beliefs, a unified Christianity was part of"[151] the Kingdom of God. No Reformer was more rocked by the breaking up of Christendom generally, and by Protestantism's breaking apart into Lutherans, Reformed believers, Baptists, etc., than was Bucer.

> "We cannot give up on those whom Christ is calling in other churches; we have to look to how we can come to an understanding with them, where we can concede to them, and what on their account we can take back for ourselves."[152]

No one worked theologically[153] as well as practically so intensively towards unity as did Bucer.[154] According to Greschat he was the "advocate

---

[149] P. D. L. Avis. "Richard Hooker and John Calvin". Journal of Ecclesiastical History 32 (1981) 1: 19-28, here p. 21.
[150] In part. N. Scott Amos. "It is Fallow Ground Here: Martin Bucer as Critic of the English Reformation". op. cit., p. 42.
[151] Reinhold Friedrich. Martin Bucer – 'Fanatiker der Einheit'? Diss.: Neuchatel, 1990. p. 195.
[152] Martin Greschat. Martin Bucer. op. cit., p. 117.
[153] Comp. Gottfried Hammann. Martin Bucer. op. cit., pp. 113-121 „Die Einheit der Kirche" and Willem van't Spijker. „De kerk in Bucers oecumensich streven". pp. 10-54 in: Frits van der Pol (ed.). Bucer en de kerk. De Groot: Kampen, 1992.
[154] See in part. Reinhold Friedrich. „Martin Bucer: Ökumene im 16. Jahrhundert". pp. 257-268 in: Christian Krieger, Marc Lienhard (ed.). Martin Bucer and Sixteenth Century Europe. vol. 1. Studies in Medieval and Reformation Thought 52. Brill: Leiden, 1993; Reinhold Friedrich. Martin Bucer – 'Fanatiker der Einheit'? op. cit.; Hartmut Joisten. Der Grenzgänger Martin Bucer: Ein deutscher Reformator. Ev. Presseverlag Pfalz: Speyer, 1991; Gottfried Bender. Die Irenik Martin Bucers in ihren Anfängen. Studia Irenica 5. Gerstenberg: Hildesheim, 1975. pp. 149-153; Otto Weber. „Die Einheit der Kirche bei Calvin". pp. 130-143 in: Jürgen Moltmann (ed.). Calvin-Studien 1959. Neukirchener Verlag: Neukirchen, 1960.

of Protestant unity."[155] For Bucer, unity was a basic requirement of the Holy Scripture as well as a personal attitude towards other Christians.[156] In his commentaries unity played a large part, whereby Ephesians 4 carried the load-bearing role.[157]

In a time of religious division, Bucer was a man of understanding, because "the tragic disfiguring separations of the Reformation had begun, and Bucer spent the largest part of his life working to overcome them."[158] Like no one else in his time, he was a promoter of reconciliation, not only within his own camp (for instance, in the dispute over the Lord's Supper between Luther and Zwingli). Bucer was also the most important partner for dialogue from the Evangelical side in religious discussions with the Roman church in 1540 and 1541 and in the contentions with Jews, Anabaptists, and religious fringe groups at that time.

> "As the advocate of unity and of the tenacious search for compromise in an epoch of contention and strife, he is the decisive trailblazer of the 1536 'Wittenberg Concord' and the most important Protestant negotiating partner in religious discussions in 1540 and 1541 with the Roman Catholic Church in Hagenau, Worms, and Regensburg. He consciously sought the whole over the parts and unity over opposition. Bucer did not belong to one church alone, but rather to ecumenism."[159]

No one at the time of the Reformation dedicated himself with such intensity to the problem of dissenting opinions as did Bucer,[160] and in doing so Martin Bucer points far beyond his own century to the present. Bucer came to be so identified with rapprochement that the Swiss Reformer Heinrich Bullinger snidely called people who sought rapprochement between the different directions among Protestants *bucerisant*.[161]

In his actions Bucer was not concerned with political coalitions or finding the lowest common denominator.

---

[155] Martin Greschat. Martin Bucer. op. cit., p. 139-171 (chapter heading).
[156] See ibid., pp. 118-119 „Einheit als persönliche Haltung".
[157] Comp. Gottfried Hammann. Martin Bucer. op. cit., pp. 113-114.
[158] Robert Stupperich. „Bucer, Martin". op. cit., p. 260.
[159] Reinhold Friedrich. „Martin Bucer". op. cit., p. 85.
[160] Comp. Gottfried Bender. Die Irenik Martin Bucers in ihren Anfängen. Studia Irenica 5. Gerstenberg: Hildesheim, 1975. pp. 149-153 „Der Gedanke der grundsätzlichen Einheit und das Problem der Duldung abweichender Meinungen".
[161] Bullinger on October 10. 1544 to Blaurer, quoted according to Willem van't Spijker. „Martin Bucer, Pietist unter den Reformatoren?". op. cit., p. 101.

"According to this firm conviction, Christians are called to resolutely pursue a consensus in significant points of teaching and ethics on the basis of Holy Scripture."[162]

In theology, "the differentiation between the tentatively-human and finally-divine goal" was important for Bucer.[163]

> "In the process, the vision of unity within Christendom constrained and drove him as it did hardly any other Reformer: 'I desire a unified church in true, pure, and constant faith in our Lord Jesus Christ. It appears to me that the only way to come to that point is to first of all and continually pray to Christ so that he gives us unity and prepares us inwardly for it. Then, gathered with the strong desire to experience his kingdom, we are to mindfully look at the fundamental aspects of faith in Christ and, if we are in agreement about them, to anchor them through common grounds. Finally, since the institutions and spiritual activities in our churches are so different, we are to recognize whether such external differences, in the light of the greater magnitude of the goal, could not somehow be made usable or at least acceptable.' No way was too distant for Martin Bucer, no hurdle too high that he would not put himself out for the unity of the church. Therefore, as the advocate of the Gospel he shifted between the defined confessions, after he had already become an envoy between parties within the Evangelical camp on the topic of the Lord's Supper. Martin Bucer was someone who crossed borders at the time of the Reformation, and today one would call him ecumenically involved and open. Certainly it was not a backward-looking ecumenism that he envisioned, that simply sought to reestablish prior circumstances in the church. On the contrary: he offered decisive resistance against that. As far as Bucer was concerned, the issue had solely to do with a renewed, Reformed church growing out of man's justification as offered in the Gospel by the grace of God alone that should yet remain one church. Many members, but one body!"[164]

As Greschat once fittingly expressed it, what identified Bucer was the "sensitivity for the moment of truth in opponents' arguments."[165]

---

[162] Gottfried Hammann. Martin Bucer. op. cit., p. 119.
[163] According to Gottfried Bender. Die Irenik Martin Bucers in ihren Anfängen. op. cit., p. 153.
[164] Hartmut Joisten. Der Grenzgänger Martin Bucer. op. cit., p. 165-166.
[165] Martin Greschat. Martin Bucer. op. cit., p. 88.

Unity through Truth

Although during his lifetime he was accused by many – with Luther leading the way – of wanting unity at any price and of having lost any clear position, to think that about Bucer is to understand him completely falsely. "He was anything other than a man seeking conciliation at any price."[166] His enormous emphasis on church discipline speaks against that. He wrote innumerable books in which he justified his view of things in a biblical-exegetical manner, and often enough he suffered for the positions he taught.

He finally let himself be driven out of his beloved Strasbourg, because he refused a compromise with the emperor.[167] In April 1548 the Augsburger Interim, an apparent agreement between the emperor and Protestants, was decreed. Initially Bucer refused to sign the document in Augsburg in April. He was thereupon detained and only released after he provided his signature. The Interim was made public in May 1548. Article 26 of the Augsburger Interim is essentially based upon Catholic teaching. However, it allowed the administration of the chalice to lay persons and allowed priests to marry. Many disputed questions of faith were simply not mentioned. What this meant practically is that the Interim was intended to recatholicize. It was not until the Peace of Augsburg that the Interim was suspended. Over time, Charles V's attempt to harmonize the differing conceptions of faith after the Schmalkaldic War, in which concessions were made to Protestants, failed due to resistance from the Catholic and the Evangelical sides.

In July 1548 Bucer composed "A Summary of Mistakes in Christian Teaching and Religion,"[168] his last work printed in German. In it he opposed the Interim and came into conflict with the council of the city of Strasbourg, which for the sake of peace yielded to the imperial ultimatum and assented to the Peace of Augsburg in February1549. In March 1549 Bucer was relieved of all of his offices in his hometown, and in April he

---

[166] Martin Greschat. Martin Bucer. op. cit., p. 88.
[167] Comp. the Vgl. die fascinating details in Reinhold Friedrich. Martin Bucer – 'Fanatiker der Einheit'? op. cit., pp. 199-209 and Andreas Gäumann. Reich Christi und Obrigkeit. op. cit., p. 120-123 and 407-419.
[168] Martin Bucer. Die letzten Straßburger Jahre 1546-149: Schriften zur Gemeindereformation und zum Augsburger Interim. published by Robert Stupperich. Martini Buceri Opera Omnia, Series I: Deutsche Schriften. vol. 17. Gütersloher Verlagshaus: Gütersloh & Presses Universitaires de France: Paris, 1981. Beginnning on p. 111; comp. the entire book on Bucer's position on the Augsburger Interim.

had to flee to England. His moral strictness and his urging for church discipline and for a core church had made him unpopular anyway.

In Bucer one finds a "spiritual openness, combined with a steadfastness when it comes to the basics."[169] Let us hear what some say regarding this. For instance, Reinhold Friedrich writes:

> "For the 'unity of the church,' however, there were also clear limits – One limit, for example, was where truth claims of the Holy Scriptures were endangered, as is found expressed in the Peace of Augsburg." "With Bucer it was never a question of peace at any price by superficial and unsustainable formulas for consensus. He was not a 'fanatic for unity,' in spite of all of the passion with which he sought to achieve the 'unity of the church.'"[170]

Martin Greschat writes:

> "It would in any case be a misunderstanding if one tries to explain Bucer's expressed readiness for dialog over these years, as well as his continual efforts to play down the Lord Supper controversy and where possible to get beyond it, by saying that he had no viewpoint of his own on this question. The opposite is the case. Since late fall 1524, Bucer had conclusively broken with the idea that in the elements of the bread and the wine the body and the blood of Christ were physically present."[171]

At another point he adds:

> "How little the still widespread picture of Bucer as a smooth strategist and verbose opportunist corresponds to reality can be conclusively seen in an impressive manner in Bucer's reaction to a document by Luther, abrasive and full of allegations, that appeared in 1533 and was addressed to people in Frankfurt. The 'apology' by the pastor in Frankfurt in March of the same year, which was composed by Bucer, argued tersely as well as reservedly. From his preliminary work on this brochure is it evident how deeply Luther's polemical work had hurt him. That he did not strike back in spite of this was in no way simply the result of tactical considerations. Rather, Bucer saw very clearly that everyone who did what they could for the cause of understanding and reconciliation in the light of the increasingly hard theological fronts in all camps immediately attracted the criticism of being innerly unsure and basically not able to be trusted in that which he taught. Bucer was prepared to expose himself to this misunderstanding. He wrote, "We at any rate have to seek unity and love towards all – God grant how they might behave towards us.'"[172]

---

[169] Gottfried Hammann. Martin Bucer. op. cit., p. 119.
[170] Reinhold Friedrich. „Martin Bucer: Ökumene im 16. Jahrhundert". op. cit., p. 268.
[171] Martin Greschat. Martin Bucer. op. cit., p. 84.
[172] Martin Greschat. Martin Bucer. op. cit., p. 111.

In the foreword to Bucer's commentary on the Gospels (*Enarrationes perpetuae in sacra quatuor evangelia*, 1530) is the following sentence:

> "If an individual wants to immediately pass sentence on someone as abandoned by the Spirit of Christ because he does not judge things exactly as you do, and if the individual is immediately ready to go up against that person as an enemy of the truth, as someone who possibly considers something false for true: whom, I ask, can one continue to consider as a brother? In any case I have never yet seen two people where each thinks exactly the same thing. And this also applies to theology."[173]

It comes down to the common Spirit and not to the letter.

In August 1532 "Of a lack of religion upon which everything depends"[174] appeared, which was Bucer's position paper on the necessity of dialogue with sectarians. He however wanted to proceed against those who did not want to be reasonable. No one was to be tolerated in Strasbourg who did not vow not to blasphemy the Christian faith.[175]

Thoughts about Election

Thoughts about election and predestination were determinative for Bucer, while there was a simultaneous emphasis on man's ethical responsibility.[176] That it did not so massively emerge as it did in Calvin or in Luther's "Bondage of the Will" has to do with Bucer's reconciliatory way of answering dissenters and not to do with weakening his teaching over against

---

[173] Quoted from the handwritten original according to Martin Greschat. Martin Bucer. op. cit., p. 105.
[174] Martin Bucer. Zur auswärtigen Wirksamkeit 1528-1533. Martini Buceri Opera Omnia, Series I: Deutsche Schriften. col. 4. E. J. Brill: Leiden, 1975. pp. 449-464.
[175] Martin Greschat. Martin Bucer. op. cit., p. 128.
[176] See the many supporting documents in Willem van't Spijker. „Prädestination bei Bucer und Calvin". pp. 85-111 in: Wilhelm H. Neuser (ed.). Calvinus Theologus. Neukirchener Verlag: Neukirchen, 1976, in part. pp. 87-102; W. Peter Stephens. The Holy Spirit in the Theology of Martin Bucer. University Press: Cambridge, 1970. pp. 23-41; W. Peter Stephens. The Holy Spirit in the Theology of Martin Bucer. op. cit., pp. 23-41; Gottfried Hammann. Martin Bucer. op. cit., pp. 134-136; Karl Koch. Studium Pietatis: Martin Bucer als Ethiker. Beiträge zur Geschichte und Lehre der Reformierten Kirche 14. Neukirchener Verlag: Neukirchen, 1962. pp. 77-90; J. W. van den Bosch. De ontwikkeling van Bucer's praedestinatiegedachjten vóór het opreden van Calvijn. Harderwijk: Mooij, 1922 (Diss. FU Amsterdam).

that of his teacher, Martin Luther, or his student in this connection, John Calvin.[177]

Bucer had a viewpoint that included the election of believers as well as the condemnation of unbelievers. He did not do this primarily due to systematic considerations. Rather, as was the case with Luther, it is particularly due to the fact that it is taught in the Holy Scriptures, namely in Paul's Letter to the Romans.[178] As far as Bucer is concerned, double predestination contradicts our reason, and a solution of the tension between human responsibility and divine sovereignty is not possible. However, it is the Holy Scripture that decides, not our thinking.[179]

Admittedly it is the case, as with Calvin, that predestination is only a special case of the fact that God works in all things. Indeed, he works in all things through his Holy Spirit.[180] He is the final authority in all that happens and claims all glory for himself.

Domiciled in the Reformed Camp

Wilhelm Neuser is surely correct that Bucer may not simply be pocketed for the Reformed camp.[181] The "range of Bucer's theology" was too broad and it influenced too many people for him to be easily pigeonholed confessionally.[182] However, on the other hand, with everything he learned from Lutherans, Anglicans, and Anabaptists, and although he never desired a confessional designation for himself, he nevertheless is clearly situated within the basic framework of a Reformed approach. Up until today he is viewed by Lutherans as Reformed.

---

[177] Comp. also Jürgen Moltmann. „Erwählung und Beharrung der Gläubigen". pp. 43-61 in: ders. (ed.). Calvin-Studien 1959. Neukirchener Verlag: Neukirchen, 1960. pp. 56-60 („Calvins Position zwischen Luther und Bucer").

[178] Also Willem van't Spijker. „Prädestination bei Bucer und Calvin". op. cit., p. 91.

[179] This description according to Karl Koch. Studium Pietatis: Martin Bucer als Ethiker. op. cit., p. 82.

[180] Karl Koch. Studium Pietatis: Martin Bucer als Ethiker. op. cit., p. 77-80.

[181] Wilhelm H. Neuser. „Bucers konfessionelle Position". pp. 693-704 in: Christian Krieger, Marc Lienhard (ed.). Martin Bucer and Sixteenth Century Europe. vol. 2. Studies in Medieval and Reformation Thought 53. Brill: Leiden, 1993.

[182] Werner Neuser. „Von Zwingli und Calvin bis zur Synode von Westminster". op. cit., p. 224. Comp. on Bucer's relationship to Zwingli H. J. Selderhuis. „Bucer en Zwingli". pp. 55-66 in: Frits van der Pol (ed.). Bucer en de kerk. De Groot: Kampen, 1992.

He also did not only strongly influence John Calvin, Anglicans, and Reformed Puritans, but the rest of the Reformed world as well. Two examples should suffice:

The 1563 Kurpfalz Order of Church Discipline, issued long after Bucer's death, had a basic structure – sin, redemption, and life – as well as additional details that were derived from Bucer's 1537 catechism.[183]

An Italian theologian, Petrus Martyr [Vermigli] (1500-1562), who like Bucer found exile in England, made a significant Calvinistic contribution to the English Reformation. He was largely defined by Bucer's thinking.

Calvin became a Calvinist through Bucer

Bucer was also of enormous importance insofar as he influenced Calvin, above all during Calvin's exile in Strasbourg. However, this influence was also exercised during a lifelong friendship.[184] One can say with J. Pannier that Calvin became a 'Calvinist' in Strasbourg.[185]

In 1538 Calvin and Farel received the order to leave the city of Geneva within three days. In September 1538 Calvin was called to the French community of exiles in Strasbourg. As far as Calvin's theological development is concerned, his time on Strasbourg was of decisive importance.

---

[183] Friedrich Lurz. Die Feier des Abendmahls nach der Kurpfälzischen Kirchenordnung von 1563. Praktische Theologie heute 38. W. Kohlhammer: Stuttgart, 1998. pp. 178-179.

[184] Comp. for the relationship between the two Marijn de Kroon. Martin Bucer und Johannes Calvin. Vandenhoeck & Ruprecht: Göttingen, 1991; Willem van't Spijker. „Bucer und Calvin". pp. 461-470 in: Christian Krieger, Marc Lienhard (ed.). Martin Bucer and Sixteenth Century Europe. vol. 1. Studies in Medieval and Reformation Thought 52. Brill: Leiden, 1993 (p. 461 further literature); Willem van't Spijker. "Bucer's Influence on Calvin, Church and Community". pp. 32-44 in: David F. Wright (ed.). Martin Bucer: Reforming Church and Society. Cambridge University Press: Cambridge, 1994; Willem van't Spijker. „Die Lehre vom Heiligen Geist bei Bucer und Calvin". pp. 73-106 in: Wilhelm H. Neuser. Calvinus Servus Christi. Ráday-ollegium: Budapest, 1988; Alexander Ganoczy, Stephan Scheld. Die Hermeneutik Calvins. Veröffentlichungen des Instituts für Europäische Geschichte, Abt. für Abendländische Religionsgeschichte 114. Steiner: Wiesbaden, 1983. pp. 76-87 Calvin und Bucer (from a Catholic point of view); Bernard Cottret. Calvin: Eine Biographie. Quell: Stuttgart, 1998. pp. 164-168; Martin Greschat. Martin Bucer. op. cit., pp. 157-158.

[185] So Willem van't Spijker. „Bucer und Calvin". op. cit., p. 470.

This is noticeable in his teaching on the different offices, his view of church discipline, liturgy, and the role of teaching on predestination.[186]

In 1539 Calvin revised and published the second edition of his *Institutes* in Strasbourg. It is evident that specifically the sections on topics such as church discipline, marriage, and others that were important for Bucer, were revised in the direction of Bucer's thinking.[187]

The reciprocal theological influence that Bucer and Calvin had[188] was based on a deep friendship and appreciation.[189] Calvin repeatedly defended Bucer against Bullinger's animosity, including the time period after Bucer's death.[190] "However, Bucer was also convinced of Calvin's extraordinary gifts and abilities."[191]

> "In all of this there was much that obviously united Bucer with Calvin, not only personally but also theologically. The emphasis on the gift of the Holy Spirit, the pressing forward toward a life full of love to one's neighbor as well as the demand for church discipline is encountered in both men. The younger found in Bucer a reliable counselor and father-like friend. In the following years this mutual trust endured quite a few stresses and crises."[192]

One of the best judges of the relationship between the two Reformers wrote the following:

> "What Calvin thought about Bucer is well-established. He expressed his thanks on many occasions, saying that he had received much from him. Very well-known is Calvin's appreciation for Bucer's abilities as a writer. According to Calvin, Bucer had, as it were, set a keystone in publishing via his studies on Romans. 'This man, who, as you know, is marked by thorough education and rich knowledge of various disciplines, has a penetrating spirit, is widely read, and possesses many other virtues is nowadays hardly exceeded by anyone and is only comparable to a few, towering above most, and is most of all worthy of praise, such that no one who reflects on it can see that

---

[186] Comp. in part. Willem van't Spijker. „Prädestination bei Bucer und Calvin". op. cit., p. 102-107.
[187] In part. Walther Köhler. Zürcher Ehegericht und Genfer Konsistorium. Bd. 2. op. cit., p. 527.
[188] Comp. Willem van't Spijker. „Prädestination bei Bucer und Calvin". op. cit., p. 85-87.
[189] Example for this in both directions compiled by Willem van't Spijker. „Bucer und Calvin". op. cit., p. 462.
[190] Willem van't Spijker. „Bucer und Calvin". op. cit., p. 465.
[191] Ibid., p. 462.
[192] Martin Greschat. Martin Bucer. op. cit., p. 158.

no one worked with more careful diligence in concerning himself with Biblical interpretation.[193]

Calvin was also professor for exegetics at the new university founded by Johannes Sturm and Martin Bucer. It was here that Calvin began to publish his Bible commentaries. Along with Bucer, Calvin participated in numerous religious discussions. In 1538 Calvin wrote an article on the Lord's Supper, in which he sought, as did Bucer, to achieve reconciliation between Zwinglians and Lutherans. However, reconciliation was not achieved.

According to Elsie Anne McKee,[194] Calvin and the Reformers gained their teaching on church discipline from the Basel Reformer Oecolampadius and from Bucer.

Calvin took the thought of differentiating between permanent and temporary offices on the basis of Ephesians 4:11 from Martin Bucer,[195] whereby Bucer admittedly did not exclude that apostles could again appear.[196] On the contrary, Calvin did not have his view of I Timothy 5:17 from Bucer.[197] Indeed, Bucer know something of a plurality of elders, but he did not have a firm list of offices as did Calvin.[198] Even so, using Romans 12:8 to refer to the office of elder is something that doubtless stemmed from Bucer.[199]

While the Reformed teaching on offices goes back to Calvin, and for this reason Reformed believers often invoke Calvin, Calvin's great estimation of the office of deacon has been almost completely forgotten.[200] Calvin

---

[193] Willem van't Spijker. „Bucer und Calvin". op. cit., p. 463.
[194] Elsie Anne McKee. Elders and the Plural Ministry: The Role of Exegetical History in Illuminating John Calvin's Theology. Travaux d'Humanisme et Renaissance Librairie 223. Droz: Genf, 1988. pp. 18-19.
[195] According to Elsie Anne McKee. Elders and the Plural Ministry: The Role of Exegetical History in Illuminating John Calvin's Theology. Travaux d'Humanisme et Renaissance Librairie 223. Droz: Genf, 1988. pp. 151-154.
[196] According to ibid., p. 188.
[197] So ibid., op. cit., pp. 97-99.
[198] Ibid., p. 125.
[199] So ibid., p. 51.
[200] In part. also Elsie Anne McKee. John Calvin on the Diaconate and Liturgical Almsgiving. op. cit., p. 13; comp., for instance, Jean Calvin. Calvin-Studienausgabe. vol. 2: Gestalt und Ordnung der Kirche. Neukirchener Verlag: Neukirchen-Vluyn, 1997. pp. 257-259 (from Ordonnances ecclésiastiqes [1541/1561] pp. 227-279).

took this appreciation from Martin Bucer[201] and came to know about it practically in Strasbourg.[202]

Exegesis Is Prior to Dogmatics

Bucer worked all his life on Biblical texts and was repeatedly prepared to listen to Holy Scripture. He did this specifically on the basis of suggestions of his opponents, regardless of stripe.

> "Bucer's theology is fundamentally Biblical. His writings are rich with Biblical quotes, his knowledge of the Holy Scriptures is extraordinary, and his exegetical achievement is impressive. The composition of his ecclesiology is never the result of a list of dogmatic premises, which he documented a posteriori with Biblical quotes, but rather it is the fruit of untiring exegetical research and reflection."[203]

In addition to the priority of exegesis over dogmatics – a typical feature of later pietism and also of the Enlightenment – practice and ethics were more important than 'pure' dogmatics:

> "Proclamation and ethics were of more value to Bucer than was unambiguous teaching. His heart beat for the interpretation of Scripture, in which he unfolded an extraordinary wealth of ideas."[204]

A Theology of Love

P. D. L. Avis finds that in addition to Bucer's emphasis on the commands of God, there is "the presence of a powerful motivation of love in his theology."[205]

---

[201] On Bucer's view of the diaconate see Gottfried Hammann. Martin Bucer. op. cit., pp. 239-242.

[202] Elsie Anne McKee. John Calvin on the Diaconate and Liturgical Almsgiving. op. cit., p. 129 and 153; comp. p. 179 reference to Bucer's document 'Von der Waren Seelsorge' from 1538. McKee names next to Bucer in ibid., p. 153 Johannes Chrysostomos as the most influential catalyst for Calvin' thoughts on the diaconate. According to ibid., pp. 185-204, and, however, following Bucer (in part. pp. 193-195), Romans 12:8 became the most important text about the diaconate, a text to which practically no expositor today refers.

[203] Gottfried Hammann. Martin Bucer. op. cit., p. 79.

[204] Werner Neuser. „Von Zwingli und Calvin bis zur Synode von Westminster". op. cit., p. 218.

Unlike any other theologian of his time, he let countless statements from both the Old and New Testaments flow into his theology. This has to be understood in order to be able to grasp his quest for the 'unity' of Christ's Church.

Love, as we have just seen, is for Bucer as for Jesus and Paul also the essence and end of the law.[206] Therefore, his entire ethic is an ethic of love.

Unity and the Lord's Supper

At the time of the Reformation, Bucer participated in practically all discussions which took place between the various Evangelical camps or between Catholics and Protestants, and he often acted as initiator, organizer, or chief negotiator.[207]

> "Within a few years Bucer had made a name for himself in Strasbourg as a zealous and able chief negotiator. There was rarely an occasion in which he was not involved."[208]

Bucer was even able to vanquish Luther's mistrust over against mediation talks and over against the Swiss. The Wittenberg Concord[209] (1536) was for Bucer a moving moment and a high point in his efforts for unity. He could not know at the time that the fracture in the Reformation would not be able to be permanently healed. "The concordat that was achieved became a milestone in ecclesiastical history."[210]

---

[205] P. D. L. Avis. "Moses and the Magistrate: A Study in the Rise of Protestant Legalism. Journal of Ecclesiastical History 26 (1975) 2: 149-172. p. 160.

[206] See the supporting documents in Karl Koch. Studium Pietatis: Martin Bucer als Ethiker. op. cit., pp. 70-73.

[207] Comp. details also in Andreas Gäumann. Reich Christi und Obrigkeit. op. cit., pp. 441-482.

[208] Robert Stupperich. „Bucer, Martin". op. cit., p. 260.

[209] Comp. Bucer's in the development of this unifying document in part. in Reinhold Friedrich. Martin Bucer – 'Fanatiker der Einheit'? op. cit., pp. 87-126, Martin Brecht. Martin Luther. vol. 3. Calwer Verlag: Stuttgart, 1987. pp. 48-67 and Martin Greschat. Martin Bucer. op. cit., pp. 142-152. The texts are found in Martin Bucer. Wittenberger Konkordie (1536). Schriften zur Wittenberger Konkordie. ed. Robert Stupperich. Martini Buceri Opera Omnia, Serie I: Deutsche Schriften. vol. 6, part 1. Gütersloher Verlagshaus: Gütersloh & Presses Universitaire de France: Paris, 1955.

[210] Wilhelm Heinrich Neuser. „Bucers Bedeutung für Kirche und Theologie heute". pp. 67-83 in: Frits van der Pol (ed.). Bucer en de kerk. De Groot: Kampen, 1992. p. 71.

Along the way Bucer never paid back Luther's frequent hostilities in kind. And it was also not incidental that it was Capito and Bucer who prepared an edition of Luther's complete works.

> "Bucer also tried to mediate in the Reformation dispute regarding the Lord's Supper:[211] Huldreich Zwingli was of the opinion that the Lord's Supper was only a symbolic action, while Luther held to a teaching that was closer to the Catholic understanding, namely that Christ is actually present in the elements of bread and wine and so gives himself to believers. In many trips Bucer endeavored to move the parties to a unified formulation. After failed negotiations at the Augsburg Reichstag in 1530, he composed his own creed, the 'Confessio Tetrapolitana,' or the 'Creed of the four cities' Strasbourg, Memmingen, Lindau and Constance. After Zwingli's death in 1531, Bucer was the head of the Upper German and Swiss Reformations; as early as 1530 he had visited Luther in the Veste Coburg castle in order to discuss a unification of the Lutheran and Upper German Reformations. Bucer's great success was the assistance with the Wittenberg Concord of 1536: the Upper German Reformers, under Bucer's lead, aligned themselves with the Lutheran viewpoint, and with that he led the southwestern area, which had been influenced by Zwingli, back to Lutheranism. His solution was 'so that all would be one,' so he fought for unity in the Reformation and against the split into Reformed and Lutheran."[212]

In doing so it is not to be thought that Bucer had no position of his own on the question of the Lord's Supper.

> "According to Bucer's conviction, Luther erred – and Bucer tried to demonstrate this with logical and exegetical arguments – when he said that all communicants actually received Christ, independent of their faith; it was also the case that the glorified Christ present in the Lord's Supper was not simply identifiable with the crucified Christ. Still, Bucer simultaneously emphasized that one could tolerate this error by the Wittenberger, because Luther no longer spoke of Christ baked in bread, but rather of his spiritual presence in the sacrament. And for Bucer that was the decisive point. That Bucer defended not only Zwingli and Oecolampadius, but also the spiritualist Schwenckfeld and in a certain way even Karlstadt, completely convinced Luther that he was correct."[213]

---

[211] Comp. as the most extensive on this Reinhold Friedrich. Martin Bucer – 'Fanatiker der Einheit'? op. cit.
[212] www.heiligenlexikon.de/BiographienM/Martin_Bucer.html (September 30, 2001).
[213] Martin Greschat. Martin Bucer. op. cit., p. 89.

In the process it is certainly appropriate to visualize the specific situation around which these discussions took place, and with this to see that the entire situation not only had a theological but also a personal side:

> "Every participant involved in this dispute was a former priest. The mass had therefore stood in the center of their churchly functions. There can be little doubt how sharply and fundamentally they then loosed themselves from this theology and that for them this topic in many respects, also emotionally, was vastly more weighty than many others. In consequence of this, everyone who took sides or sought their own angle knew each other or were even befriended with each other, especially in southwest Germany. Due to common spiritual and personal agreement, they were therefore were always informed about convictions and reservations that slowly formed here and there in other camps."[214]

A typical example of Bucer's interest in peace among Christians is the dispute regarding bishop's vestments in England. John Hooper did not want to be inducted as a bishop in traditional vestments. Archbishop Cranmer called upon Bucer, and Bucer criticized both sides. There were more important problems than questions of dress, namely congregational theological training and spiritual standards[215] – and this was the case even though he had spoken out against liturgical vestments his whole life long.[216]

The Cologne Reformation

These talks also included religious discussions with the Catholic side. Bucer also fought there[217] for a unity based on Holy Scripture and vehemently called for a joint council to clarify the problem. Bucer's attempts to not only call for talks but also to bring about a council count as last efforts to prevent a break-up of the churches before the Council of Trent finally decided against the Protestant side. On account of this, a Catholic historian of the council calls him the "apostle of harmony."[218] Admittedly the religious

---

[214] Martin Greschat. Martin Bucer. op. cit., p. 83.
[215] Comp. details in Hartmut Joisten. Der Grenzgänger Martin Bucer. op. cit., pp. 157-158; Andreas Gäumann. Reich Christi und Obrigkeit. op. cit., p. 125 und Martin Greschat. Martin Bucer. op. cit., p. 244.
[216] Comp. ibid., pp. 75-76.
[217] Comp. details in Amy N. Burnett. The Yoke of Christ. op. cit., pp. 122-142; Martin Greschat. Martin Bucer. op. cit., pp. 177-192 and Andreas Gäumann. Reich Christi und Obrigkeit. op. cit., pp. 449-482.
[218] Hubert Jedin. A History of the Council of Trent. vol. 1: The Struggle for the Council. Herder: St. Louis (USA), 1957. p. 362, Annotation 2.

discussions ended with a unity of coercion in the form of the Augsburg Interim, the rejection of which forced the flight from Strasbourg.

These so-called religious discussions had a long history for Bucer. Already in 1521, as Franz von Sickingen's chaplain, he was to moderate secret negotiations between Luther and Jean Glapion, the confessor of Emperor Charles V. Bucer held long discussions with Glapion.[219]

Calvin was one of the few theologians, who, along with Bucer, sought every last opportunity for understanding with Catholic theologians as well as a unification of Evangelical churches.[220] (Bucer coined the term 'syncretism,' which later received another definition).

Even more conspicuously visible was Bucer's readiness to take unusual paths, at first as the only Reformer to help the Cologne Archbishop Hermann von Wied in planning a Reformation which did not involve officially changing over to Protestantism. Later Bucer was able to gain Melanchthon's[221] support for the efforts in Cologne. Bucer worked out a program during his time in Bonn, which was the archbishop's seat of government, of how a complete church could maintain its external form while reforming itself from within.[222] Even when this attempt failed after one and one-half

---

[219] See details in Martin Brecht. Martin Luther. Vol. 1. op. cit., pp. 428-429.

[220] Also Otto Weber. „Die Einheit der Kirche bei Calvin". pp. 130-143 in: Jürgen Moltmann (ed.). Calvin-Studien 1959. Neukirchener Verlag: Neukirchen, 1960. p. 130.

[221] Comp. to relationship between Bucer and Melanchthon: Heinz Scheible. „Melanchthon und Bucer". pp. 369-394 Christian Krieger, Marc Lienhard (ed.). Martin Bucer and Sixteenth Century Europe. vol. 1. Studies in Medieval and Reformation Thought 52. Brill: Leiden, 1993; Jürgen Diestelmann. Actio Sacramentalis: Die Verwaltung des Heiligen Abendmahles nach den Prinzipien Martin Luthers in der Zeit bis zur Konkordienformel. Luth. Buchhandlung H. Harms: Groß Oesingen, 1996. pp. 87-97.

[222] Comp. to attempt at Cologne Reformation, Martin Bucer et al. Schriften zur Kölner Reformation. published by Gottfried Seebaß. Martini Buceri Opera Omnia, Series I: Deutsche Schriften. vol. 2. Gütersloher Verlagshaus: Gütersloh & Presses Universitaire de France: Paris, 1999; Mechthild Köhn. Martin Bucers Entwurf einer Reformation des Erzstiftes Köln: Untersuchung der Entstehungsgeschichte und der Theologie des 'Einfältigen Bedenckens' von 1543. Untersuchungen zur Kirchengeschichte 2. Luther-Verlag: Witten, 1966; Marijn de Kroon. „Bucer und die Kölner Reformation". pp. 493-506 and Heinz Scheible. „Melanchthon und Bucer". pp. 369-394 in: Christian Krieger, Marc Lienhard (ed.). Martin Bucer and Sixteenth Century Europe. vol. 2. Studies in Medieval and Reformation Thought 53. Brill: Leiden, 1993; 450 Jahre Kölner Reformationsversuch: Katalog zur Ausstellung im Historischen Archiv Köln. Kölner Ökumenische Beiträge 28. Stallberg Verlag: Alfter, 1993 (in part. on Bucer pp. 35-39); Andreas Gäumann. Reich Christi and Obrigkeit. op. cit., pp. 483-500; Amy N. Burnett. The Yoke of Christ. op. cit., pp. 143-162; Martin Greschat. Martin Bucer. op. cit., pp. 192-200; Has-

years by force of arms, historically it was still of great importance. This was due to the fact that it became a model for the Reformation of the Anglican Church in England. It is no surprise that in England significant portions of the liturgy, of educational concepts, and other elements were taken from Bucer's Cologne-Bonn writings.

By the way, Protestantism in the Bonn area continued for a long time in individual congregations and in the underground.[223]

The Role of the Church Fathers

Above all when looking at Bucer's countless activities, one can easily forget that he was a highly educated man, for whom it was no accident that he concluded his life with a professorship in Cambridge.

> "The most scholarly book that Bucer wrote was his commentary on Romans. He must have worked on it for many years. The scholastic training of the composer is highly evident in it."[224]

Bucer's education is also expressed in the fact that he worked through innumerable documents both past and present by friends and foes.

> "In his interpretative work Bucer held close to the text. His method of interpretation is to a large extent determined by patristics. His knowledge of ancient and medieval interpreters is astonishingly broad. The authority of the Holy Scriptures is paramount."[225]

As far as interpretation is concerned, Chrysostom and Augustine ranked foremost[226] with Bucer. The role the Church Fathers played, which is significant as far as Bucer is concerned[227] is, however, to be understood

---

tings Eells. Martin Bucer. op. cit., pp. 321-337; from older literature: Carl Varrentrapp. Hermann v. Wied und sein Reformationsversuch in Köln. Duncker & Humblot: Leipzig, 1878; Carl Varrentrapp. „Zur Charakteristik Hermann von Wied, Bucers und Groppers". Sonderdruck aus Zeitschrift für Kirchengeschichte 20 (1900) 1: 38-58.

[223] Thomas P. Becker. „Gegenreformation und protestantische Bewegung im Bonner Raum (1547-1595)". Bonner Geschichtsblätter 39 (1989): 31-60 = http://members.aol.com/tombee/gegrefbn.html (17.2.2001).
[224] Robert Stupperich. „Bucer, Martin". op. cit., p. 265.
[225] Robert Stupperich. „Bucer, Martin". op. cit., p. 266.
[226] Also Karl Koch. Studium Pietatis: Martin Bucer als Ethiker. op. cit., p. 36.
[227] Irena Backus. "Martin Bucer and the Patristic Tradition". pp. 55-70 in: Christian Krieger, Marc Lienhard (ed.). Martin Bucer and Sixteenth Century Europe. vol. 1.

against the background of Bucer's conception of tradition.²²⁸ Although Bucer was a Biblical theologian and had dogmatic exegesis as a priority, the tradition of the early church did not have an absolute, but rather a relative value. He only turned away from it when the Holy Scriptures forbid him, but not as a matter of principle.

Bucer Was Internationally Active

Bucer's activities knew no national or cultural borders. Among the Reformers, such a position was otherwise only found with Calvin. Bucer had, unlike hardly any other theologian of his time, a European vision: beyond the Alsace and Germany he maintained connections with Italy, Bohemia, Denmark, Sweden, Poland and as far as Palestine and fostered the Reformation in France and England.²²⁹ Bucer was the 'border crosser of the Reformation,' a mediator between denominations and nations, a champion of what we today understand as ecumenism. Hartmut Joisten writes:

> "Martin Bucer was not only a border crosser between camps within the church. He also crossed borders between the various religions of Europe. Not only the Reformation in Germany, Switzerland, and England received impetuses from him, but the Waldensians in Italy, the Bohemian Brethren in Czechoslovakia, and the Protestants in Sweden. In the course of this European interaction, Bucer developed a fine sense of the fact that every region of Europe had its own history and its own features, and that these distinctives could not be taken away. 'Reconciled differences' is the way one could designate his motto in European affairs. He did not foresee uniformity or some sort of leveling down."²³⁰

Studies in Medieval and Reformation Thought 52. Brill: Leiden, 1993; Gottfried Hammann. Martin Bucer. op. cit., pp. 314-317.

[228] See on this in part. Gottfried Hammann. Martin Bucer. op. cit., pp. 39-40 and 103-113.

[229] Comp. for example contributions relating to Bucer's relationship to France, England, Scotland, Sweden, Poland, and Italian in Christian Krieger, Marc Lienhard (ed.). Martin Bucer and Sixteenth Century Europe. vol. 2. Studies in Medieval and Reformation Thought 53. Brill: Leiden, 1993. Regarding the relationships to the Netherlands comp. Willem F. Dankbaar. Martin Bucers Beziehungen zu den Niederlanden. Kerkhistorische Studien 9. Nijhoff: Den Haag, 1961 (on pp. 55-57 translations of Bucer's writings in Dutch are listed) and – including the effects beyond Bucer's death – B. J. Spruyt. „De irenische Bucer in de polemiek tussen Remonstranten en Contra-Remonstranten". pp. 84-174 in: Frits van der Pol (ed.). Bucer en de kerk. De Groot: Kampen, 1992.

[230] Hartmut Joisten. Der Grenzgänger Martin Bucer. op. cit., p. 172.

Martin Greschat describes it similarly:

> "Bucer's view and goal, insofar as it had become clear, had for years gone far beyond Strasbourg, beyond the Protestant camp, and not least of all beyond the Empire itself. He had connections in Italy as well as in the Netherlands, in northern Germany and up into Denmark, in Silesia and in the surrounding areas. Naturally, these were in many cases only very loose, although mostly very targeted personal relationships that nonetheless were far from influencing these people in his interests or in the interests of the type that marked the Strasbourg Reformation during those years. However, it is undeniable that Bucer's thinking took on a truly European breadth that likewise made him soar beyond many other Reformation theologians. Not least of all, as a result of this, many of his generous as well as controversial hard and fast pronouncements can now be explained . . ."[231]

Bucer wanted the Kingdom of God to expand and have more than a local impact. For this reason "he could only see Strasbourg as a beachhead for the expansion of the Gospel and the penetration of the Kingdom of God."[232] This becomes clearer still when we speak about Bucer and world missions. The fact that Bucer took on the great challenge in England at the age he did is typical for him.

> "Bucer was still one of the most important and most highly revered personalities in the Evangelical camp. This is not least of all expressed in the numerous offers of asylum that he received from 1547 onwards. These included invitations from Melanchthon in Wittenberg and from Calvin in Geneva. When, in spite of this, Bucer decided for England, his conviction was that his particular experiences and abilities could most reasonably and most fruitfully be utilized in a country in which the Reformation appeared to be prevailing victoriously."[233]

From Bucer's European efforts we move to global efforts and thoughts on missions:

> "That Martin Bucer was the only one among the Reformers whose ministry and concerns were applied on a European level is widely recognized. To designate him as a European Reformer is correct insofar as his sphere of influence extended over the entire European occident. If one asks about motivation, then what emerges is that Bucer's thinking and actions were predominantly oriented towards all of Christendom. He is therefore a European

---

[231] Martin Greschat. Martin Bucer. op. cit., p. 115.
[232] Martin Greschat. Martin Bucer. op. cit., p. 103.
[233] Martin Greschat. Martin Bucer. op. cit., p. 232.

insofar as in the 16th century Christendom was principally coextensive with Europe. To renew a person through faith and in this manner to bring him closer to the Kingdom of God was Bucer's desire, not only for Strasbourg as a free imperial city (*Reichsstadt*) and not only for the German Reich, but rather for all people. Bucer's global consciousness is in our opinion unique for the time of the Reformation and deserves closer investigation."[234]

A Proponent of World Missions Not Befitting His Time

Bucer appears outright modern when it comes to his advocacy of world missions.[235] He was the only Reformer for whom the Great Commission was still in force[236] and for whom the expansion of the Gospel beyond the Christian world was also a matter of course. "Because Bucer was filled with the missionary thought of spreading the *regnum Christi* as far as possible, his thoughts and efforts went far beyond Strasbourg."[237]

"Mission (in the sense that it has been understood since the 18th century) is for him a component of the pastoral office of the church. Its expansion over the entire earth belongs to its essence. He expressed himself clearly in 1538 with his explanation of the various aspects of the churchly office, but this concern is found much earlier in his writings. In his interpretation of the Lord's Prayer (1527) he exhorted believers to ask God "to expand the borders of his kingdom to all deathly poor creatures." With regard to this progressive extension, the power of the Spirit is apportioned to believers, with

---

[234] Christian Krieger, Marc Lienhard (ed.). Martin Bucer and Sixteenth Century Europe. vol. 2. Studies in Medieval and Reformation Thought 53. Brill: Leiden, 1993. p. 477.

[235] The most important investigations relating to this are: Walter Holsten. „Christentum und nichtchristliche Religion nach der Auffassung Bucers". pp. 9-72 in: Walter Holsten. Das Evangelium und die Völker: Beiträge zur Geschichte und Theorie der Mission: Goßnersche Mission: Berlin, 1939, in part. pp. 189-194 [originally: Theologische Studien und Kritiken 107 (1936): 105-194]; Gottfried Hammann. Martin Bucer. : 1491-1551. Zwischen Volkskirche und Bekenntnisgemeinschaft. Veröffentlichungen des Instituts für Europäische Geschichte 139. Steiner: Stuttgart, 1989. pp. 121-126 (Section „Die Kirche als missionarische Gemeinschaft"); Heinrich Frick. Die evangelische Mission: Ursprung, Geschichte, Ziel. Bücherei der Kultur und Geschichte 26. Schröder: Bonn, 1922. pp. 41-44; comp. Otto Michaelis. „Zur Frage des Missionsverständnisses der Reformatoren". Zeitschrift für Missionskunde und Religionswissenschaft 41 (1926): 337-343.

[236] Also Paul D. L. Avis. The Church in the Theology of the Reformers. Marshall Morgan & Scott: London, 1981. p. 175.

[237] Andreas Gäumann. Reich Christi und Obrigkeit. op. cit., p. 423.

which they accomplish things more wondrous than Christ himself. The missionary zeal of the church provides witness to the presence and dynamic nature of the Holy Spirit. And this task is similarly a basis for the apostolic calling and for the coming of Christ."[238]

The central portion of his writings that relate to missions is found in a famous section of his "On True Pastoral Care,"[239] in which he not only obligated the church to world missions, but also obligated each individual Christian who must support the church while it conducts missions. In doing so it is clear that Bucer, in particular through the conquest of the New World, became aware of the issues of missions. He condemned the aggressive methods of the Spanish and called instead for evangelism that conformed to the lordship of Christ through the Holy Spirit.[240]

Central portions on world missions are found in Bucer's programmatic church writings. Walter Holsten brought together many pieces of evidence from Bucer's Bible commentaries, primarily from his commentaries on Zephaniah, Romans, the Psalms, and the gospels.[241]

Against this background Bucer occupied himself with true knowledge in philosophy and paganism, and he accepted such thought only insofar as it was in accord with the Holy Scriptures,[242] with the idea of natural revelation,[243] with Judaism,[244] Islam,[245] and non-Christian religions[246] in general.

(Bucer's recommended anti-Jewish policy for Hessen,[247] dating from December 1538, speaks a completely different language, similar to Luther.)

The Influence of His Liturgy

Some of Bucer's specific thoughts and foundational ideas were formative for liturgies within completely different denominations and countries.[248]

---

[238] Gottfried Hammann. Martin Bucer. op. cit., p. 125.
[239] Martin Bucer. Schriften der Jahre 1538-1539. Martin Bucers Deutsche Schriften. vol. 7. Published by Robert Stupperich. Gütersloher Verlagshaus: Gütersloh; Presses Universitaires de France: Paris, 1964. pp. 151-153.
[240] All ibid.
[241] Walter Holsten. „Christentum und nichtchristliche Religion nach der Auffassung Bucers". op. cit., pp. 190-191.
[242] Ibid., p. 163-168.
[243] Ibid., p. 142-153.
[244] Ibid., p. 179-186.
[245] Ibid., p. 186-189.
[246] Ibid., p. 152.
[247] Andreas Gäumann. Reich Christi und Obrigkeit. op. cit., p. 511-526.

Calvin's Order of Worship for Geneva (1542) had its roots in the simplified mass in the Strasbourg Liturgy[249] and is indeed in large sections taken literally from Bucer.[250] The great influence that Bucer had on church order in Cologne and on many later *censura* will be addressed shortly. The thought of a weekly Lord's Supper – indeed only for true followers of Jesus – was passed on by Bucer to many, for instance to Calvin.[251] This occurred when Bucer, as Calvin, was not able to put it into practice anywhere other than England.

In large part Archbishop Cranmer took the English Book of Common Prayer from the church order of Cologne,[252] and the same goes for confirmation and marriage rites. The church order of Cologne (*Reformationsbedenken, or Reformation Concerns*) was translated very soon into English and became well known in England. Cranmer's most important liturgical consultants in addition to Bucer were two Reformed theologians who were strongly influenced by Bucer, Petrus Martyr and John Hooper.[253] Cranmer's first liturgy displays so few changes over against the Cologne program that the 'First Book of Prayer' was also seen as a translation of Bucer's Cologne liturgy.[254] When a revision of this book was undertaken, Bucer's opinion, the 'Censura,' was available. Due to missing documents, it will remain unclear how much influence this second book, written for Cranmer, actually had on the 'Second Common Book of Prayer.' At least one is able to say with Peter Thiede:

---

[248] The most comprehensive investigations on Bucer's understanding of liturgy remains Gerrit Jan van de Poll. Martin Bucer's Liturgical Ideas. Diss. Groningen, 1957.

[249] Jean Calvin. Calvin-Studienausgabe. vol. 2: Gestalt und Ordnung der Kirche. Neukirchener Verlag: Neukirchen-Vluyn, 1997. pp. 137-225 „Genfer Gottesdienstordnung (1542) mit ihren Nachbartexten", sowie Andreas Marti in der „Einführung". pp. 137-143, here p. 137.

[250] Also Robert Stupperich. „Bucer, Martin". op. cit., p. 262.

[251] Also ibid., p. 137 and Gerrit Jan van de Poll. Martin Bucer's Liturgical Ideas. op. cit., p. 138.

[252] For instance also Samuel Leuenberger. Cultus Ancilla Scripturae: Das Book of Common Prayer als erweckliche Liturgie – ein Vermächtnis des Puritanismus. op. cit., pp. 4-5; Hastings Eells. Martin Bucer. op. cit., p. 411; Constantin Hopf. Martin Bucer and the English Reformation. op. cit., p. 94. The standard work on this is still Edward C. Whitaker. Martin Bucer and the Book of Common Prayer. Alcuin Club Collections 55. Mayhew-McCrimmon: Great Wakering, 1974 standard work.

[253] According to Samuel Leuenberger. Cultus Ancilla Scripturaea. op. cit., p. 15.

[254] In part. according to Hastings Eells. Martin Bucer. op. cit., p. 411.

". . . . in 1552 under Edward VI there was a revision of the 'Prayer Book,' in which not least thanks to Martin Bucer's influence, even stronger, typically Reformed formulations were in the meantime incorporated."[255]

In his liturgical thought Bucer was particularly independent. Unlike Luther and Calvin, he held that the laying on of hands, for instance, was not only allowed, but rather important within the Church congregation, for ordination as well as for the sick or for other blessings.[256] The fact that he also anchored the Ten Commandments in the worship service, not however as an indictment (law) but rather after the forgiveness of sins as a form of praise and of showing the way for the life of the Christian (gospel), was typical and original.[257]

Bucer's Social Ethic

Bucer made enormous achievements in the area of social ethics and wanted to reform the church and society through schools[258] and training centers.

In the process he was very optimistic and hardly defined by Luther's thought that the last days of history and of the antichrist had come. Greg L. Bahnsen even calls Bucer – somewhat anachronistically but from his tendency correct – a postmillennial[259] and points out that Bucer shared this positive view of the expansion of the Kingdom of God with many Re-

---

[255] Carsten Peter Thiede. Religion in England. Gütersloher Taschenbücher 635. Gütersloher Verlagshaus: Gütersloh, 1994. p. 103.
[256] Gerrit Jan van de Poll. Martin Bucer's Liturgical Ideas. op. cit., pp. 71-72.
[257] Ibid., p. 75.
[258] Ernst-Wilhelm Kohls. Die Schule bei Martin Bucer in ihrem Verhältnis zu Kirche und Obrigkeit. Pädagogische Forschungen 22. Quelle & Meyer: Heidelberg, 1963.
[259] All Greg L. Bahnsen. "The Prima Facie Acceptability of Postmillennialism". The Journal of Christian Reconstruction 3 (1976/77) 2 (Winter): Symposium on the Millennium. pp. 48-105. p. 76.

formed theologians.²⁶⁰ Even today Reformed theologians such as Georg Huntemann identify with Bucer's optimistic eschatology.²⁶¹

Shortly before his death Bucer wrote "On the Reign of Christ" (*De regno Christi*),²⁶² a comprehensive societal and ecclesiastical reform program for the Church of England.

A Critical Partner of the State

Karl Koch assumes that Bucer did not separate spiritual and worldly authorities into a two kingdoms doctrine as did Luther,²⁶³ but rather saw both kingdoms under Christ's lordship. However, he himself wrote that, in Bucer, one sees that worldly authority was exclusively responsible for external peace and the spiritual profession was exclusively responsible for the inner man.²⁶⁴ Apart from that, Luther also viewed the state as under the lordship of God. Bucer assumed, as did Luther, a Christian state, but in the

---

[260] For the history of Reformed postmillennialism comp. "The Reformed Heritage of Postmillennialism". pp. 68-104 in: Greg L. Bahnsen. "The Prima Facie Acceptability of Postmillennialism". op. cit.; Gary DeMar, Peter J. Leithart. The Reduction of Christianity: Dave Hunt's Theology of Cultural Surrender. Dominion Press: Ft. Worth (TX), American Vision Press: Atlanta (GA), 1988. pp. 229-270; Joseph R. Balyeat. Babylon: The Great City of Revelation. Onward Press: Sevierville (MI), 1991. pp. 9 and 42-43; on Puritan Postmillennialism: Gary North (ed.). Journal of Christian Reconstruction 6 (1979) 1 (Summer): Symposium on Puritanism and Progress.

[261] Comp. Georg Huntemann. Der verlorene Maßstab: Gottes Gebot im Chaos dieser Zeit. Verlag der Liebenzeller Mission: Bad Liebenzell, 1983. p. 131; comp. pp. 131-135.

[262] Latin text: Martin Bucer. De regno Christi libri 2 (1550). Published by Francois Wendel. Martini Buceri Opera Omnia, Series I: Opera Latina. vol. 15, part 1. Gütersloher Verlagshaus: Gütersloh & Presses Universitaire de France: Paris, 1955 and Martin Bucer. Du royaume de Jésus-Christ (1558). ed. Francois Wendel. Martini Buceri Opera Omnia, Series I: Opera Latina. vol. 15, part 2. Gütersloher Verlagshaus: Gütersloh & Presses Universitaire de France: Paris, 1954; German original: Martin Butzer. Vom Reich Christi unsers Herren und Heiland ... Verteudscht von Israelem Achacivm. Wendel Rihel: Straßburg, 1563. 514 pp.; also: Martin Butzer. Christliche Reformation. Samuel Emmel: Straßburg, 1568; modern English translation: Martin Bucer. „De Regno Christi". pp. 155-394 in: Wilhelm Pauck (ed.). Melanchthon and Bucer. The Library of Christian Classics: Ichthus Edition. The Westminster Press: Philadelphia (PA), 1969, Westminster John Knox Press: ibid., 1997^Pb; comp. the summary in Martin Greschat. Martin Bucer. op. cit., pp. 246-252.

[263] Karl Koch. Studium Pietatis. op. cit., p. 153.

[264] Ibid., 155.

practical separation of duties and responsibilities, he went much further than Luther and even somewhat beyond Calvin.

What is striking is Bucer's repeated strong criticism of authorities, because they interfered too much in the office of the church, or because they did nothing against the immoral state of affairs.[265]

> "Bucer's theology is of pre-eminent relevance for the relationship between the church and the state. On the one hand, he tried to maintain freedom from the authorities for the Evangelical church and free-church efforts, and his impact on pietism in the 17th and 18th centuries has this as its basis. On the other hand, he insistently emphasized the meaning of Christian tradition for the entire society."[266]

It is often held that Martin Bucer associated the civil law of the Old Testament with the present day state,[267] above all in his writing entitled 'On the Reign of Christ' (*De Regno Christi*). As a matter of fact, for Bucer the Old Testament's moral and civil law was largely still valid,[268] and the enforcement of sentences was still in force.[269] He also saw this to be the case for

---

[265] See, for example, Walther Köhler. Zürcher Ehegericht und Genfer Konsistorium. vol. 2. op. cit., p. 486.

[266] www.heiligenlexikon.de/BiographienM/Martin_Bucer.html (30.9.2001).

[267] For example James B. Jordan. "Calvinism and 'The Judicial Law of Moses'. op. cit., pp. 23-25; John Graham Child. Biblical Law in the Theology of R. J. Rushdoony: A Systematic Theological Analysis and Appreciation. Master of Theology. University of South Africa, 1986. p. 7 under reference to P. J. Verdam. Mosaic Law in Practice and Study Throughout the Ages. J. H. Kok: Kampen (NL), 1959. p. 9; Gary North. Unconditional Surrender: God's Program for Victory. Geneva Divinity School Press: Tyler (TX), 1987 2nd ed. pp. 340-341; Douglas F. Kelly. The Emergence of Liberty in the Modern World: The Influence of Calvin on Five Governments from the 16th Through 18th Centuries. Presbyterian and Reformed: Phillipsburgh (NJ), 1992. pp. 21-22; comp. the printed Bucer texts in Gary North (ed.). The Journal of Christian Reconstruction 5 (1978/1979) 2 (Winter): Symposium on Puritanism and Law.

[268] Also Marijn de Kroon. Martin Bucer und Johannes Calvin. Vandenhoeck & Ruprecht: Göttingen, 1991. pp. 163-167 and Wilhelm Pauck. Das Reich auf Erden: Utopie und Wirklichkeit: Eine Untersuchung zu Butzers 'De Regno Christi' und zur englischen Staatskirche des 16. Jahrhunderts. Arbeiten zur Kirchengeschichte 10. Walter de Gruyter: Berlin, 1928. pp. 45-49 and 60-67.

[269] Also Marijn de Kroon. Studien zu Martin Bucers Obrigkeitsverständnis: Evangelisches Ethos und politisches Engagement. Gütersloher Verlagshaus. Gerd Mohn: Gütersloh, 1984. pp. 17 and 29-36 and often, and Wilhelm Pauck. Das Reich auf Erden. op. cit., pp. 45 and 48.

religious offenses[270], such as the death penalty for adultery,[271] even though he wanted to abstain from stoning.[272] For Bucer, all laws had to be measured against God's law.[273] Bucer had a clear "Conception of a Christian State,"[274] which rested upon a "Christocracy."[275]

There is, however, also another viewpoint that Bucer held. In his important study regarding Bucer's ethics, Karl Koch assumes that for Bucer the civil law had basically been abolished.[276] In this connection Wilhelm Pauck writes:

> "Although for Christians the *civilia legis mosaicae decreta* no longer has any validity, namely with respect to the circumstances for which they were given, their *proprius finis* is still binding. In particular this applies to the commandments which have to do with the state's necessary discipline."[277]

How do we resolve this contradiction? In my opinion Bucer supports[278] Calvin's position,[279] the position taken by the Westminster Confession, and the view taken as well by Philipp Jacob Spener.[280] This is the view that the Old Testament civil law is indeed no longer valid. However, the view also says that in spite of this there is something valuable regarding wisdom and goodness contained in the Old Testament shell that one can feasibly inte-

---

[270] Marijn de Kroon. Studien zu Martin Bucers Obrigkeitsverständnis. op. cit., pp. 29-36 and 144 and 149 and often.
[271] Wilhelm Pauck. Das Reich auf Erden. op. cit., p. 46.
[272] Marijn de Kroon. Martin Bucer und Johannes Calvin. op. cit., p. 165.
[273] Wilhelm Pauck. Das Reich auf Erden. op. cit., p. 45.
[274] Wilhelm Pauck. "Martin Bucer's Conception of a Christian State". Princeton Theological Review 2 (1928) 80-88.
[275] According to Wilhelm Pauck. Das Reich auf Erden. op. cit., p. 65.
[276] Karl Koch. Studium Pietatis: Martin Bucer als Ethiker. Beiträge zur Geschichte und Lehre der Reformierten Kirche 14. Neukirchener Verlag: Neukirchen, 1962. pp. 68-69.
[277] Wilhelm Pauck. Das Reich auf Erden. op. cit., p. 48.
[278] Also Walter Holsten. „Christentum und nichtchristliche Religion nach der Auffassung Bucers". op. cit., p. 108.
[279] For an assessment of the civil law among Reformers see P. D. L. Avis. "Moses and the Magistrate: A Study in the Rise of Protestant Legalism. Journal of Ecclesiastical History 26 (1975) 2: 149-172 (pp. 151-156 Luther, pp. 157-160 Melanchthon, pp. 160-162, Bucer, pp. 163-164 Calvin, pp. 166-171 Anglican and Scottish theologians).
[280] Philipp Jacob Spener. Speners Katechismuserklärung: D. Philipp Jacob Speners Erklärung der christlichen Lehre nach der Ordnung des Kleines Katechismus Dr. Martin Luthers. Missionsverlag der Evangelisch-Lutherischen Gebetsgemeinschaften: Bielefeld, 1984 (1677/1702). pp. 22-27 (Questions 22-33).

A Critical Partner of the State 73

grate into one's thoughts.[281] For Calvin the civil law was abolished, but it was repeatedly used as a source of wisdom.[282] For Bucer, the Old Testament civil laws are beneficial[283] but not compulsory.[284] Spener describes his view as follows:

> "Is the Jewish worldly law still applicable to us?: 'No; because it was only given to the Jews and to their law enforcement officials and therefore ends with them. It is, however, still open to Christian authorities to introduce that which the wisest legislator has decreed for his own people, if they think it could be of use to them. Apart from that, it is advisable for us to obey the laws and ordinances of the authorities under which we live."[285]

The technical term for this point of view is the 'equity' of Old Testament civil law (Greek *epieikeia*, Latin *aequitas*). The judicial concept 'equity' means "the modification of a given rule of law for the purpose of its reasonable adaptation to a specific case."[286] With this concept it is not Bucer but rather Lutheran orthodoxy or the 1647 Reformed Westminster Confession that sees the civil law of the Old Testament as repealed and still useful as a source of wisdom:

> "God also gave Israel various civil laws as a political body, which together with the state of this people were discontinued and now no longer obligate anyone, other than calling for general equity [or: correspondence]."[287]

---

[281] Comp. to discussion in Thomas Schirrmacher. Anfang und Ende von 'Christian Reconstruction' 1959-1995: Geschichte, Theologie und Aufsplitterung einer reformierten Bewegung in den USA. VKW: Bonn, 2001. pp. 210-267 und Thomas Schirrmacher. Ethik. 3 vols. VTR: Nürnberg & RVB: Hamburg, 2001 2 nd ed. vol. 1. pp. 481-493 and more fundamentally vol. 3. pp. 558-791.

[282] So ebd. S. 163ff

[283] H. J. Selderhuis. „Die hermeneutisch-theologische Grundlage der Auffassungen Bucers zur Ehescheidung". a. a. O. S. 238

[284] Vgl. die gute Darstellung bei Andreas Gäumann. Reich Christi und Obrigkeit. a. a. O. S. 218-222, welche alttestamentlichen Gesetze nach Bucer noch gelten und welche nicht.

[285] Philipp Jacob Spener. Speners Katechismuserklärung. a. a. O. Ebd. S. 23

[286] Gustav Wingren. „Billigkeit". S. 642-645 in: Gerhard Müller (Hg.). Theologische Realenzyklopädie. Bd. 6. de Gruyter: Berlin, 1993/1980 (Studienausgabe), hier S. 642. Wingren beschreibt nur die griechische und die lutherische Sicht.

[287] Thomas Schirrmacher. der evangelische Glaube kompakt: Das Westminster Bekenntnis ... Hänssler: Neuhausen, 1998. p. 139 (Art. 19.4.) – Art. 19.3. speaks about the abrogation of the ceremonial law. Art. 19.5. says: "The moral law binds all people at all times to obedience, both those who are justified and those who are not. The obligation to obey the moral law is not only because of its content, but also because of the authority of God the Creator, who gave it. In the gospel, Christ

To which extent Spener or the Westminster Confession was directly or indirectly influenced by Calvin and Bucer at this point is worthy of investigation.

Groundbreaking and Innovative Ethics in Detail

Bucer's ethics were also in their detail often marked by sound exegesis and were very innovative and groundbreaking for later centuries.

It was first Martin Bucer[288] and John Calvin who brought the view back into the church that interest was allowed, while usurious interest and exploitation of the poor was forbidden.[289]

It is striking that among the Reformers Bucer's work ethic,[290] because it did not primarily come from feudalism and the given layers of society ('Standesdenken'), but rather assumed that every individual should pursue his avocation according to ability, affinity, and with a certain ardor.[291]

Marriage Is a Love Partnership

Bucer's view of marriage is striking due to the fact that it went far beyond his time[292] in seeing the love partnership between man and woman. His

---

in no way dissolves this obligation, but greatly strengthens it" (ibid., pp. 139-140). Translators note: English translation of Art. 19.5 is from the Westminster Confession of Faith, Modern English Study Version, available on http://opc.org/documents/MESV_frames.html and accessed August 5, 2009.

[288] Georg Klingenburg. Das Verhältnis Calvins zu Butzer: untersucht auf Grund der wirtschaftsethischen Bedeutung beider Reformatoren. Diss. Carl Georgi: Bonn, 1912. pp. 22-41.

[289] Supporting documents in Rousas John Rushdoony. Institutes of Biblical Law. Presbyterian and Reformed: Phillipsburg (NJ), 1973. pp. 474-475 and Gerhard Simon. „Bibel und Börse: Die religiösen Wurzeln des Kapitalismus". Archiv für Kulturgeschichte 66 (1984): 87-115.

[290] See all of Karl Koch. Studium Pietatis: Martin Bucer als Ethiker. op. cit., pp. 115-124.

[291] See ibid, p. 115.

[292] The most important investigations regarding Bucer's views on marriage and divorce are: H. J. Selderhuis. Marriage and Divorce in the Thought of Martin Bucer. Sixteenth Century Essays and Studies 48. Thomas Jefferson Univ. Press: Kirksville (IL), 1999 [Niederländisches Original: H. J. Selderhuis. Huwelijk en echtscheiding bij Martin Bucer. J. J. Groen en Zoon: Leiden, 1994]; H. J. Selderhuis. „Martin Bucer und die Ehe". pp. 173-184 in: Christian Krieger, Marc Lienhard (ed.).

view was too progressive[293] to enjoy approval. Bucer had married two years prior to Luther and matched up active and, for the most part, successful women with Reformers, such as with Capito and Calvin.[294]

In connection with the question of the purpose of marriage and contraception, I have shown in another context that the traditional Catholic teaching on marriage up until the 19th century always placed reproduction in the first position and in principle does this until today. The Protestant teaching on marriage began with Luther to hesitantly put the relationship between the marriage partners at the fore, even if it was not until the 20th century, based on advanced knowledge about procreation, that forbiddance of contraception loosened.[295] Present day teaching on marriage by most Protestants who hold to the Holy Scriptures is, however, already clearly found in Martin Bucer.

Martin Bucer may have been the first person to classically present the later Evangelical view with his notion that the principal purpose of marriage is a "unity and alliance of soul and body."[296] The marriage that was founded prior to the fall of man[297] had an external and an internal side, but the inner side is the more important one, that is, the deep will that both want to live for each other.[298] For this reason, it is not like the Catholic

---

Martin Bucer and Sixteenth Century Europe. Bd. 1. Studies in Medieval and Reformation Thought 52. Brill: Leiden, 1993; H. J. Selderhuis. „Die hermeneutisch-theologische Grundlage der Auffassungen Bucers zur Ehescheidung". pp. 229-243 in: Willem van't Spijker (ed.). Calvin: Erbe und Auftrag: Festschrift für Wilhelm Heinrich Neuser zum 65. Geburtstag. Kok: Kampen, 1991; Francois Wendel. Le mariage à Strasbourg à l'époque de la réforme 1520-1692. Collection d'études sur l'histoire du droit et des institutions de l'Alsace 4. Impr. Alsacienne: Straßburg, 1928; Constantin Hopf. Martin Bucer and the English Reformation. Basil Blackwell: Oxford, 1946. pp. 107-115; Walther Köhler. Zürcher Ehegericht und Genfer Konsistorium. vol. 2: Das Ehe- und Sittengericht in den süddeutschen Reichsstädten, dem Herzogtum Württemberg und in Genf. Quellen und Abhandlungen zur Schweizerischen Reformationsgeschichte. II. Series, vol. X. M. Heinsius: Leipzig, 1942. pp. 386-487 (pp. 349-504 on Strasbourg at large).

[293] In part. Constantin Hopf. Martin Bucer and the English Reformation. op. cit., pp. 107-115.
[294] Comp. H. J. Selderhuis. Marriage and Divorce in the Thought of Martin Bucer. op. cit., pp. 128-137.
[295] See Thomas Schirrmacher. Ethik. 3 vols. VTR: Nürnberg & RVB: Hamburg, 2001 2nd ed. vol. 2. pp. 735-770.
[296] Maurice E. Schild. „Ehe/Eherecht/Ehescheidung VII. Reformationszeit". pp. 404-346 in: Gerhard Müller (ed.). Theologische Realenzyklopädie. vol. 9. de Gruyter: Berlin, 1993/1982 (Studienausgabe), here p. 343.
[297] H. J. Selderhuis. „Martin Bucer und die Ehe". op. cit., p. 180.
[298] Ibid., p. 179.

view, where children, and sexuality as a means of bringing about children, have the top priority. Rather, the top priority goes to *fides* (trust) and *communio* (the loving partnership) between the marriage partners.[299] Thus the wife is valued very highly by Bucer.[300] Therefore, Bucer cannot accept that mostly women are the ones who suffer in bad marriages.

> "So it is in Bucers writings on marriage that we find definitions of marriage, and the most exhaustive definition is that in *De Regno Christi*: the true marriage, as God has implemented it, and as how he wills that it be valued, is the alliance between man and wife, which obligates both to mutually play a role in the life of the other and indeed in an alliance that encompasses divine as well as human law. In addition, they give each other their bodies and do so in sexual relations as this necessarily arises. All of this should be done in the greatest willingness and love, whereby the man demonstrates what it is to be the head of the woman, just as Christ is the head of the church, and the wife submits to the husband as the church submits to Christ."[301]

A New View of Divorce

All of the thoughts mentioned also had consequences for Bucer's view on divorce.

> "He captured a concept of marital companionship in which Erasmus' concerns were deepened. Bucer's deliberations greatly transcended his time and had truly revolutionary features. Bucer not only accepted adultery as a reason for divorce, but rather the hopeless disintegration of this alliance – and indeed for the wife as well as for the husband. 'The service of marriage is not something that can be exacted by force [. . .] For that reason attention is to be paid that one does not dare want to be wiser than God himself, who desires that those be divorced who do not have one heart together.'"[302]

Martin Bucer spent a large portion of his Latin magnum opus *De Regno Christi* ('The Reign of Christ')[303] shortly before his death on the question of marriage, divorce, and remarriage. In it he assumed that marriage could be dissolved when the union of marriage was physically or spiritually bro-

---

[299] Ibid., p. 180.
[300] Ibid., p. 182.
[301] Ibid., p. 177.
[302] Martin Greschat. Martin Bucer. Ibid., p. 127.
[303] The editions are mentioned above in detail.

ken, that is to say, no longer extant.³⁰⁴ He is the only pre-modern theologian known to me who also allowed divorce in the case of brutal violence and cruelty on the part of the husband.³⁰⁵ Alongside this he named malicious desertion, refusal of marital duties, dishonorable guilt, and irremediable ailments that inhibit marriage as reasons for divorce.

Bucer's view was primarily made known a century later by John Milton, when Milton set out a rather freely translated and abridged English version³⁰⁶ of his own arguments and documents over against the prevailing marital law found within canon law.

Many other Reformers fundamentally represented the opinion that divorce was only acceptable in the case of adultery, only to then go and accept other grounds in specific cases.³⁰⁷ Calvin, for instance, represented the narrower view in his commentaries, but in his suggestion for marital law in Geneva he allowed other grounds for divorce.³⁰⁸

Apart from that the Reformers – as in other questions – borrowed from the Church Father Aurelius Augustine, who assumed that in Matthew 19:9

---

[304] Comp. Constantin Hopf. Martin Bucer and the English Reformation. Basil Blackwell: Oxford, 1946. pp. 107-115; Karl Koch. Studium Pietatis: Martin Bucer als Ethiker. op. cit., pp. 125-152; Wilhem Pauck. Das Reich auf Erden: Utopie und Wirklichkeit: eine Untersuchung zu Butzers 'De Regno Christi' und zur englischen Staatskirche des 16. Jahrhunderts. Arbeiten zur Kirchengeschichte 10. Walter de Gruyter: Berlin, 1928. p. 34; Hastings Eells. Martin Bucer. op. cit., pp. 122-126; Jeffrey R. Watt. "The Marriage Laws Calvin Drafted for Geneva". pp. 245-255 in: Wilhelm H. Neuser (ed.). Calvinus Sacrae Scripturae Professor. W. B. Eerdmans: Grand Rapids (MI), 1994. pp. 253-254.

[305] Ibid., pp. 253-254 and Maurice E. Schild. „Ehe/Eherecht/Ehescheidung VII. Reformationszeit". pp. 404-346 in: Gerhard Müller (ed.). Theologische Realenzyklopädie. vol. 9. de Gruyter: Berlin, 1993/1982 (study edition), here p. 343.

[306] Above all 'The Doctrine and Discipline of Divorce' (1642). pp. 221-356 in John Milton. Complete Prose Works of John Milton. vol. 2. Yale University Press: New Haven (USA) & Oxford University Press: London, 1959 (in part. pp. 242-244: Appealing to Moses, pp. 245-247: every covenant can draw to a close; pp. 261-268 1 Corinthians 7 as an Argument; pp. 268-269 Divorce not only due to adultery; pp. 273-274 the protection of life is more important than the marriage; pp. 329-337 on the gospel texts) and the numerous editions of 'The Argument for Divorce' in ibid. Comp. with these editions Ernest Sirluck. "Introduction". pp. 1-216 in: ibid., pp. 145-158. Ibid. pp. 137-143 Sirluck also demonstrates, that Milton's divorce at the time of the first composition was not able to be foreseen; rather, he was still happily married. John Milton strongly followed Hugo Grotius in his interpretation of New Testament texts on divorce (in part. pp. 329-337).

[307] Wilhem Pauck. Das Reich auf Erden. op. cit., p. 34.

[308] Comp. Jeffrey R. Watt. "The Marriage Laws Calvin Drafted for Geneva". op. cit., pp. 251-252 and the entire contribution.

not only physical but also spiritual adultery was meant, whereby he declared the acceptability of divorce from unbelievers.[309]

It is important to emphasize that Bucer came to his views on marriage and divorce on exegetical grounds.[310] Karl Koch writes the following:

> "Every aspect of Bucer's notion of divorce is supported by Bible passages. The sole norm for Bucer is the Holy Scripture." He is not interested in a string of Bible verses that are used to prove a biased position, but rather a conscientious investigation of the Bible."[311]

In my "Ethics" work, on the basis of exegetical and Biblical-theological arguments, I expressly campaign for Bucer's view of marriage and divorce.[312] It is for this reason that I would not like to address this question in any more detail here. The fact is, however, that Bucer is closer to the current day thinking of most Protestants and Evangelicals who identify with the Holy Scriptures than anyone else from the 16th to the 19th century.

The Tragedy of the Bigamy of Philipp von Hessen

Still to be mentioned is Bucer's (and Luther's) peculiar attitude toward polygamy and the permission (*Beichtrat*) granted to the Landgraf Philipp von Hessen to secretly marry a second wife.[313] This is to avoid an impression

---

[309] According to Henri Crouzel. „Ehe/Eherecht/Ehescheidung V. Alte Kirche". pp. 325-330 in: Gerhard Müller (ed.). Theologische Realenzyklopädie. vol. 9. de Gruyter: Berlin, 1993/1982 (Studienausgabe), here p. 329 (with a list of references).

[310] In part. H. J. Selderhuis. „Die hermeneutisch-theologische Grundlage der Auffassungen Bucers zur Ehescheidung". op. cit., pp. 229-230; H. J. Selderhuis. Marriage and Divorce in the Thought of Martin Bucer. op. cit. and already Karl Koch. Studium Pietatis. op. cit., pp. 143-145.

[311] Both H. J. Selderhuis. „Die hermeneutisch-theologische Grundlage der Auffassungen Bucers zur Ehescheidung". op. cit., p. 230.

[312] Thomas Schirrmacher. Ethik. 3 vols. VTR: Nürnberg & RVB: Hamburg, 2001 2nd ed. vol. 2. pp. 609-630.

[313] Comp. to Bucer's opinions on Henry VIII and Philipp von Hessen's bigamy in Andreas Gäumann. Reich Christi und Obrigkeit. op. cit., pp. 526-537; Hastings Eells. Martin Bucer. op. cit., pp. 256-269; Johannes Müller. Martin Bucers Hermeneutik. Quellen und Forschungen zur Reformationsgeschichte 32. Mohn: Gütersloh, 1965. pp. 252-256; Martin Greschat. Martin Bucer. op. cit., pp. 169-171; Karl Koch. Studium Pietatis: Martin Bucer als Ethiker. op. cit., pp. 150-151; Constantin Hopf. Martin Bucer and the English Reformation. op. cit., pp. 195-198; H. J. Sel-

The Tragedy of the Bigamy of Philipp von Hessen

that Bucer is to be glorified and the unpleasing sides of his activities concealed. It was namely, as Andreas accurately remarked, a "strong backlash against constructing the *regnum Christi*."[314]

Since, however, I have addressed Bucer's and Luther's *Beichtrat* in my writings on ethics,[315] what I want to do here is limit myself to a short overview. At the beginning of 1539 Martin Bucer, Philipp Melanchthon, and Martin Luther negotiated about the Hessian Landgraf Philipp von Hessen's desire to marry a second woman.[316] Melanchthon, in the name of all three, composed the *Beichtrat*.[317] Luther was the first to sign, which he did on December 10, 1539, and later many leading Hessian clergymen also added their signatures. Subsequently, the Landgraf married his 17-year-old concubine Margarete von der Sale on March 4, 1540[318] as his second wife. Martin Bucer and Philipp Melanchthon were groomsmen,[319] although bigamy was of late punishable with death under imperial law. As a result, the Wittenberg theologians were politically, completely entangled in the whole affair.[320]

Bucer argued fully for monogamy. He approved of Phillip von Hesse's bigamy for one reason, namely in order to prevent a greater fornication. If the electoral prince was unable to control himself and was not to be deterred from having a relationship in addition to that with his unloved wife, then it was better that he be in a polygamous relationship than to have an extramarital relationship.

---

derhuis. Marriage and Divorce in the Thought of Martin Bucer. op. cit., pp. 137-148 (Henry VIII) and pp. 149-161 (Philipp von Hessen).

[314] Andreas Gäumann. Reich Christi und Obrigkeit. op. cit., p. 526.

[315] Thomas Schirrmacher. Ethik. 3 vols. VTR: Nürnberg & RVB: Hamburg, 2001². vol. 2. pp. 803-817.

[316] The most comprehensive presentation of the Landgrave of Hessen's bigamy is William Walker Rockwell. Die Doppelehe des Landgrafen Philipp von Hessen. N. G. Elwert'sche Verlagsbuchhandlung: Marburg, 1904. In addition the following are important: Wilhelm Maurer. „Luther und die Doppelehe Landgraf Philipps von Hessen". Luther: Mitteilungen der Luthergesellschaft 24 (1953): 97-120 und Martin Brecht. Martin Luther. Bd. 3. Calwer Verlag: Stuttgart, 1987. pp. 205-214.

[317] Wilhelm Maurer. „Luther und die Doppelehe Landgraf Philipps von Hessen". op. cit., p. 97.

[318] Ibid., pp. 100-101.

[319] Martin Brecht. Martin Luther. vol. 3. op. cit., p. 206.

[320] Comp. August Fürnohr. Die Todesstrafe in ihrer rechtshistorischen Entwicklung in Deutschland bis zur Carolina. Jur. Diss.: Erlangen, 1909. p. 147 on Charles V's embarrassing court code, or *Halsgerichtsordnung*.

Bucer as a Role Model for Our Time

In many ways, Bucer was far advanced for his time and therein is an enduring role model for us[321], as noted:
- As a theologian of the Holy Spirit
- In his early commitment to world missions
- In his effort to speak with all those who were errant, and in spite of everything to try and win them over with the Scriptures in his hand
- In his certainty that we all make mistakes and are never theologically unflawed
- In the distinction between basics of the faith that cannot be surrendered and less important theological points of view
- In the energy with which he combined unambiguous theological convictions with always listening to those who think differently
- In teaching that diversity does not automatically contradict unity
- In repeated energetic attempts to bring movement to deadlocked positions such as the question of baptism
- In emphasizing love in ethics
- In emphasizing that forensic justification and change in our lives through the sanctification of the Holy Spirit are not contradictions but rather belong together
- In emphasizing that ethics based on commands are to be complemented by situational ethics
- In emphasizing the love relationship as the core of marriage
- In seizing upon the New Testament meaning of small groups alongside the larger church
- In creatively structural answers to challenges of the times (e.g., in confirmation)
- In his critical attitude towards the state
- And in his call for a church that is free from state leadership

A Discussion of Three New Important Dissertations on Martin Bucer

In addition to the solid and comprehensive biography on Bucer by Martin Greschat,[322] which at the present time provides the best overview of Bucer

---

[321] See also the list in Gottfried Hammann. Martin Bucer. op. cit., pp. 338-341.

A Discussion of Three New Important Dissertations on Martin Bucer 81

and the questions and research problems that relate to him, it is above all dissertations which have been moving Bucer research forward with great leaps for somewhat more than two decades. Dissertations have also, to some extent, provided new pictures of Bucer.

These circumstances result in a situation where increasingly French[323] and Dutch[324] dissertations are translated into German and English, sometimes ten years later, that has brought about a new international standard and interchange. That such an exhaustive and important dissertation as that composed by Reinhold Friedrich in Switzerland regarding Bucer's role in the negotiations for agreement in the dispute over the Lord's Supper[325] is still unpublished after ten years shows however, that Bucer is treated as a stepmother in research in comparison to Luther or Melanchthon, for instance.

In the following the newest Bucer dissertations will be discussed. They are a Swiss work dating from 2001 related to Bucer's political ethics, a 1999 English translation of a 1994 Dutch dissertation regarding Bucer's marital and sexual ethics, and an American dissertation from 1994 regarding Bucer's understanding of pastoral care and church discipline.

Andreas Gäumann. Reich Christi und Obrigkeit: Eine Studie zum reformatorischen Denken und Handeln Martin Bucers. Zürcher Beiträge zur Reformationsgeschichte 20. Peter Lang: Bern, 2001. ISBN 3-906766-75-6. 584 pp.

Andreas Gäumann is the author of a dissertation presented in 2000 at the University of Neuenberg (Switzerland), which is fascinating to read and is a supremely informed and richly documented presentation of large portions of Bucer's ethics As such, it serves to finally supersede Karl Koch's one-sided and flawed portrayal.[326] Gäumann assumes correctly that

---

[322] Martin Greschat. Martin Bucer: Ein Reformator und seine Zeit. C. H. Beck: München, 1990.
[323] For example Gottfried Hammann. Martin Bucer: 1491-1551. Zwischen Volkskirche und Bekenntnisgemeinschaft. Veröffentlichungen des Instituts für Europäische Geschichte 139. Steiner: Stuttgart, 1989 (French original Entre la secte e la cite, 1984).
[324] For example Willem van't Spijker. The Ecclesiastical Office in the Thought of Martin Bucer. Studies in Medieval and Reformation Thought 57. Brill: Leiden, 1996 (Dutch De ambten bij Martin Bucer. Diss. Amsterdam, 1970); comp. the dissertation by H. J. Selderhuis discussed below.
[325] Reinhold Friedrich. Martin Bucer – 'Fanatiker der Einheit'? Diss.: Neuchatel, 1990.
[326] Karl Koch. Studium Pietatis: Martin Bucer als Ethiker. Beiträge zur Geschichte und Lehre der Reformierten Kirche 14. Neukirchener Verlag: Neukirchen, 1962.

the 'Kingdom of Christ' and its realization in the life of the individual Christian, of the church, and of the state is Bucer's ruling theme. Hence, Gäumann portrays Bucer's political ethics on chosen topics and events and relates them to Bucer's overall teaching and ministry.

Even if one asks the question why Gäumann does not immediately dare to give an overall presentation of the Bucer's theology or at least of Bucer's ethics, I would estimate that he covers roughly 70-80%. Such a result is a large step for Bucer research. Gäumann presents Bucer's self-conception and how he appears in the source documents, not primarily from a confessional point of view. Koch, for instance, saw Bucer as a student of Erasmus and as a humanist, who never correctly understood Luther's theology of the cross. But surely Bucer was everything other than a humanist and cannot be placed in any denominational pigeon-hole, even when he tends toward the Reformed sphere more than the Lutheran. Specifically, because he did not start a denomination or help fashion one, his concerns first of all have to be presented on their own before they are measured against Luther, Zwingli, or Calvin. Bucer's emphasis on the Holy Spirit in all areas of dogmatics and practical theology is certainly without parallel in the 16th century, yet its warrant has to be measured against the Protestant principle regarding the Holy Scriptures and not some proportional representation of a denomination. Gäumann is superbly successful in this effort.

In his first chapter, Gäumann (pp. 21-33) describes the state of research and evaluates practically all important works and essays from recent decades, which (in my opinion) is an overview of current literature on Bucer. In the second chapter (pp. 43-127), Bucer's life is traced chronologically, whereby the theological and ethical topics that are in the foreground are indeed central. The result is a certain repetition with later, more exhaustive treatment.

Chapter three (pp.129-256) investigates – coherently for the first time as far as I know – what Bucer understood by the term *regnum Christi* and how it could become a reality. "In the center of this research work is Bucer's central term *regnum Christi*" (p.38).

At this point Bucer's teaching is placed over against Bucer's practice, namely in chapter four, what he was able to put into practice in Strasbourg (pp. 259-314), and in chapter five (pp. 315-420) where he failed there. Subsequently, chapter six (pp. 425-538) similarly discusses Bucer's ministry outside of Strasbourg, namely in Hesse, the Electorate of Cologne, and England.

The high points of this research work are, in my opinion, the presentation of Bucer's teaching on the Holy Spirit (pp. 143-158), on good works (pp. 174-187), and on pastoral care and church discipline (pp. 359-406). As far as Bucer's practical ministry is concerned, the sections about his interaction with dissidents (pp. 326-358), Anabaptists (pp. 504-510), and Jews (pp. 511-525), as well as his role in the dispute over the Lord's Supper (pp. 444-448), religious discussions (pp. 449-482), in the Cologne Reformation (pp. 483-500), and in the Augsburger Interim (pp. 407-420) are noteworthy. When Gäumann, however, gives a comprehensive opinion (and correctly a critical one) regarding Bucer's view on Phillip von Hesse's bigamy (pp. 526-538) under the heading "A strong backlash in constructing the *regnum Christi*" (pp. 526), one might have expected that Bucer's actual teaching on marriage would have been presented at another place in more detail, in a manner similar to how he was favorably assessed by Selderhuis.

H. J. Selderhuis. Marriage and Divorce in the Thought of Martin Bucer. Sixteenth Century Essays and Studies 48. Thomas Jefferson Univ. Press / Truman State University Press [http://tsup.truman.edu]: Kirksville (IL), 1999. ISBN 0-943549-68-X. 406 pp.

While the Dutch dissertation of his doctoral advisor, the renowned Bucer researcher Willem van't Spijker,[327] took 26 years until an English translation, produced in 1996[328], began to have its impact, Selderhuis' dissertation[329] needed only five years. Two of Selderhuis' preliminary works had already given a foretaste of the first comprehensive presentation of Bucer's teaching on marriage, which dispensed with viewing Bucer through the prejudiced glasses of prior centuries or by comparing him to other Reformers.

As Selderhuis sees it, Bucer's teaching on marriage is above all the result of his Biblical studies and one undertaken in order to produce a comprehensive substitute for the Catholic canonical marital law. This was an exercise that no other Reformer dedicated himself to and for which no other Reformer thanked him.

Selderhuis begins with an overview of the state of research on the topic (pp. 1-3). He considers it a catastrophe, since neither in the literature regarding marital law nor in Bucer literature is there appropriate appreciation for Bucer's comprehensive writings and ministry. When mentioned, it is done in the form of prejudices about the 16th century and not on the basis of sources which have to a large extent only recently become accessible.

---

[327] Willem van't Spijker. De ambten bij Martin Bucer. Diss. Amsterdam, 1970.
[328] Willem van't Spijker. The Ecclesiastical Office in the Thought of Martin Bucer. Studies in Medieval and Reformation Thought 57. Brill: Leiden, 1996.
[329] H. J. Selderhuis. Huwelijk en echtscheiding bij Martin Bucer. J. J. Groen en Zoon: Leiden, 1994.

The negative 16th century reactions (pp. 360-372) to Bucer's teaching on marriage are explicable for Selderhuis. Since, however, Bucer's teaching on marriage both claims to be arise out of Holy Scripture and to largely correspond to current Protestant teaching on marriage that is bound to Scripture, one should not spread further rumors but rather realize that Bucer simply came several centuries too soon.

To begin with, Selderhuis presents the status of canonical marital law and all its problems in the 16th century (pp. 9-31). One can agree with Selderhuis that Bucer's efforts are only able to be understood upon this background. In addition, a summary is made of what other Reformers wanted to put in the place of canonical church law (pp. 32-50). However, why approximately one-half of the summary is dedicated to Heinrich Bullinger (pp. 43-50) is not understandable.

After that, as in practically all dissertations on Bucer, his biography is first of all recounted, even if there is a certain focus on questions of celibacy and writings on marriage (pp. 51-115). In my opinion this part could have been omitted. Thereafter there is a section about Bucer's own two marriages (pp. 116-128), which were of central significance for Bucer. After all that can be said, Bucer was not only the first to make marital love, fellowship, and partnership the first purpose of marriage, but he achieved this ideal in both of his marriages. Apart from that, the first purpose of marriage had always been producing descendants.

A chapter on Bucer's influence on other marriages adroitly follows Bucer's own marital history (pp. 128-164). Bucer was not only one of the first Reformers to marry. He also battled so that others could marry and in so doing became a weighty marriage broker (pp. 128-137). His tragic opinions on Henry VIII's and Philipp of Hesse's bigamous behavior conclude this section (pp. 137-164).

It is not until the second half of the paper that the actual core, a systematic presentation of Bucer's teaching on the topic of marriage (pp. 165-353), is put forth. Within three topical areas, marriage's beginnings and essence (pp. 165-256), among others, are treated as 'positive' aspects, while thereafter the 'negative aspect' in the form of the problematic nature of divorce (pp. 257-326) and the dispute regarding celibacy (pp. 327-353) are handled.

Marriage is for Bucer the cornerstone of society. This is due to the fact that it leads individuals from self-love to love of neighbor, which is the prerequisite for church and state. He did not take the purpose of marriage from tradition, which says that the purpose of marriage is to produce descendants and to prevent fornication. A change in this tradition began indeed with Luther and Calvin, but they only mitigated the tradition and did not surmount it. To a greater degree, Bucer sees the central and primary purpose of marriage in the creation account and in the Holy Scriptures in marital love, in fellowship, and yes, even if in the framework of the 16th century, in partnership, since it is not good that man be alone and the counsel of a woman be missing.

Accordingly, sexuality first of all does not serve to conceive descendants, but it rather serves marital fellowship and joy. For this reason, Bucer sees marriage without sexuality as unthinkable and an abandonment of the sexual relationship as a sign of the death of a marriage. He rejects the prohibition on divorce, since the Holy Scriptures speak of divorce and indeed not only in cases of adultery. Rather, the Holy Scriptures speaks of divorce in other cases that mean an end of a marriage, for instance as Paul describes or as otherwise described in the Old Testament. Divorce is always objectionable. However, for the sake of the hardness of the human heart, it is from God, and often it is the only way out as a reaction to sin that has occurred. Divorce should not destroy a marriage, but rather testify that in essence a marriage is no longer at hand. That Bucer assumes a uniform teaching on marriage and divorce in both the Old and the New Testaments becomes increasingly clear as the discussion progresses.

Since the point is to determine whether a marriage still exists, Bucer allows divorce if the husband has obligated himself as a mercenary and removes himself from the family. This was a widespread problem at that time. Since the husband no longer wants to continue the marriage, and the marital fellowship *de facto* no longer exists due to many years' separation, it is better for the wife to call for divorce and to remarry than to enter into an extramarital relationship or to end up without her or the children being provided for.

Generally Bucer believes that the wife is the one who suffers under the prohibition on divorce. He also believes that the prohibition against remarriage adds more to fornication than if the one who is left or betrayed remarries and can express their sexuality in acceptable surroundings.

Selderhuis' dissertation is a milestone in Bucer research. Bucer is not only the author of the first 'modern' teaching on pastoral care, but rather also the first person who made an attempt to replace the great vacuum in practical lifestyle questions that came with the abolishment of canonical church law. The attempt at this replacement occurred with life principles drawn from Holy Scripture with respect to the shape and structure of marriage and family, of work, and of the church.

Amy N. Burnett. The Yoke of Christ: Martin Bucer and Christian Discipline. Sixteenth Century Essays and Studies 26. Sixteenth Century Jour-

nal Publ. / Truman State University Press [hrrp://tsup.truman.edu]: Kirksville (MO), 1994. ISBN 0-940474-28-X. 244 pp.

After Amy Nelson Burnett drew attention to herself with several essays that showed how closely tied Bucer's understandings of pastoral care and church discipline were with other 'trademarks' such as confirmation or discussions with Anabaptists,[330] there finally followed a complete dissertation presented to the Northeast Missouri State University on Bucer's understanding of church discipline in theory and practice. The dissertation, which was produced on the basis of extensive archival research in France, Switzerland, and Germany, is now available in a revised version.

The work is put together in tight chronological form and goes from Bucer's first, early opinion from 1529 (p. 55) to his late work shortly before his death, which is the Reformation program for the Church of England (especially pp. 208-216).

Two aspects are significant in addition to the minutia of historical reconstruction. Firstly, Bucer's most prominent teaching and ecclesiopolitical 'trademarks' are all very closely woven together and are dependent on each other. This applies to confirmation, pneumatology, ethics, the vital, small house church (pp. 180-207) within the framework of large churches, lay elders, the emphasis on pastoral care, and church discipline. In all of these things what one is dealing with is that through the power of the Holy Spirit in the life of the individual, the kingdom of God is realized. Also, through the pastoral care of each for the other, which can especially occur with the assistance of lay elders and pastors, individuals are strengthened, and the will of God is better understood and more consistently followed.

On the other hand, Bucer's teaching on church discipline is actually pastoral care (in particular pp. 87-121). Exclusion from the church community, which we normally place in connection with the concept of 'church discipline,' seldom remains an *ultima ratio,* or last resort (in particular p.221). It in no way leaves the tempted, the half-hearted, and doubting ones without help.

As much as Bucer (unfortunately) still drew upon the assistance of state authorities in order to achieve the will of God in the individual, so much was this type of pastoral care for him the quintessential task of the church community and of each Christian gifted by the Spirit. For this reason Bucer built a bridge between the state church concept of the Lutheran and Re-

---

[330] For example Amy Nelson Burnett. "Martin Bucer and the Anabaptist Conflict of Evangelical Confirmation". Mennonite Quarterly Review 68 (1994): 95-122; Ann Nelson Burnett. "Church Discipline and Moral Reformation in the Thought of Martin Bucer". Sixteenth Century Journal 22 (1991): 439-456.

formed Reformation and the Anabaptist free church concept. He did this since he wanted to bind the community of believers with the church. Believers pursue sanctification. The church is there for everyone and looks after societal concerns. This is in my opinion a concept that up to the present day points the way forward, and thanks to such research papers, it is increasingly being brought out of the shadows of history and out of prejudice-laden historiography.

About the Author

Books by Thomas Schirrmacher in chronological order (With short commentaries)

For a full book list see www.thomasschirrmacher.net/eine-seite/books-published.

Selection from the author's books:

Theodor Christlieb und seine Missionstheologie. Verlag der Evangelischen Gesellschaft für Deutschland: Wuppertal, 1985. 308 pp.

[Theodor Christlieb and his theology of mission] *A study of the biography, theology and missiology of the leading German Pietist, professor of practical theology and international missions leader in the second half of the nineteenth century.*

Marxismus: Opium für das Volk? Schwengeler: Berneck (CH), 1990[1], 1997[2]. 150 pp.

[Marxism: Opiate for the People?] *Marxism is proven to be a religion and an opiate for the masses. Empasizes the differences between Marxist and Biblical work ethics.*

Paul in Conflict with the Veil!? VTR: Nürnberg, 2002[1]; 2007[2]. 130 pp.

Exegetical examination of 1. Corinthians 11,2-16, following an alternative view of John Lightfoot, member of the Westminster assembly in the 16th century.

Ethik. Neuhausen: Hänssler, 1994[1]. 2 vol. 883 & 889 pp.; Hamburg: RVB & Nürnberg: VTR, 2001[2]. 3 vol. 2150 pp.; 2002[3], 2009[4]; 2011[5]. 8 volumes. 2850 pp.

[Ethics] *Major Evangelical ethics in German covering all aspects of general, special, persocial and public ethics.*

Legends About the Galilei-Affair. RVB International: Hamburg, 2001[1]; 2008.[2]. 120 pp.

Law or Spirit? An Alternative View of Galatians. RVB International: Hamburg, 2001[1]; 2008.[2]. 160 pp.

This commentary emphasising the ethical aspects of Galatians wants to prove that Galatians is not only fighting legalists but also a second party of Paul's opponents, who were totally opposed to the Old Testament and the Law.

God Wants You to Learn, Labour and Love. Reformation Books: Hamburg, 1999. 120 pp.

Four essays for Third World Christian Leaders on Learning with Jesus, Work Ethic, Love and Law and Social Involvement.

World Mission – Heart of Christianity. RVB International: Hamburg, 1999[1]; 2008.[2]. 120 pp.

Articles on the Biblical and systematic fundament of World Mission, especially on mission as rooted in God's being, on 'Mission in the OT', and 'Romans as a Charter for World Mission'.

Human Rights Threatened in Europe: Euthanasia – Abortion – Bioethicconvention. RVB International: Hamburg, 2001[1]; 2008.[2]. 100 pp.

Updated Lectures on euthanasia and biomedicine at the 1st European Right to Life Forum Berlin, 1998, and articles on abortion.

Be Keen to Get Going: William Careys Theology. RVB: Hamburg, 2001¹; 2008². 64 pp.

First discussion of Carey's theology in length, explaining his Calvinistic and Postmillenial backround.

Love is the Fulfillment of Love – Essays in Ethics. RVB: Hamburg, 2001¹; 2008.². 140 pp.

Essays on ethical topics, including role of the Law, work ethics, and European Union.

Mission und der Kampf um die Menschenrechte. RVB: Hamburg, 2001. 108 S.

[Mission and the Battle for Human Rights] *The relationship of world missions and the fight for human rights is discussed on an ethical level (theology of human rights) as well as on a practical level.*

The Persecution of Christians Concerns Us All: Towards a Theology of Martyrdom. At the same time Idea-Dokumentation 15/99 E. VKW: Bonn, 2001. 156 pp.

70 thesis on persecution and martyrdom, written for the International Day of Prayer for the Persecuted Church on behalf of the German and European Evangelical Alliance

Hope for Europe: 66 Theses. VTR: Nürnberg, 2002

Official thesis and study of hope in the Old and New Testament for Hope for Europe of the European Ev. Alliance and Lausanne Europe. Also available in German, Czech, Dutch, Spanish, Romanian, Portuguese, French, Russian, Italian, Hungarian, Latvian.

Thomas Schirrmacher, Christine Schirrmacher u. a. Harenberg Lexikon der Religionen. Harenberg Verlag: Düsseldorf, 2002. 1020 pp.

[Harenberg Dictionary of World Religions] In a major secular dictionary on world religions, Thomas Schirrmacher wrote the section on Christianity ('Lexicon of Christianity', pp. 8-267) and Christine Schirrmacher the section on Islam ('Lexicon of Islam', 'pp. 428-549).

Studies in Church Leadership: New Testament Church Structure – Paul and His Coworkers – An Alternative Theological Education – A Critique of Catholic Canon Law. VKW: Bonn, 2003¹; RVB: Hamburg, 2008.². 112 pp.

Hitlers Kriegsreligion: Die Verankerung der Weltanschauung Hitlers in seiner religiösen Begrifflichkeit und seinem Gottesbild. 2 vol. VKW: Bonn, 2007. 1220 pp.

[Hitlers Religion of War] *A research about the religious terms and thoughts in all texts and speeches of Hitler of Hitler, pleading for a new way of explaining Hitler's worldview, rise and breakdown.*

Moderne Väter: Weder Waschlappen, noch Despot. Hänssler: Holzgerlingen, 2007. 96 pp.

[Modern Fathers] Presents the result of international father research, explains the necessity of the father's involvement for his children and gives practical guidelines.

Internetpornografie. Hänssler: Holzgerlingen, 2008. 156 pp.

[Internet pornography] *Intense study of spread of pornography, its use amongst children and young people,* its *psychological results and dangers, including steps how to escape sex and pornography addiction.*

May a Christian Go to Court and other Essays on Persecution vs. Religious Freedom. WEA Global Issues Series. VKW: Bonn, 2008. 120 pp.

Essays: "Is Involvement in the Fight Against the Persecution of Christians Solely for the Benefit of Christians?", "But with gentleness and respect: Why missions should be ruled by ethics". "May a Christian Go to Court?", "Putting Rumors to Rest", "Human Rights and Christian Faith", "There Has to Be a Social Ethic".

Indulgences: A History of Theology and Reality of Indulgences and Purgatory. VKW: Bonn, 2011. 164 pp.

History and theology of the Catholic view on indulgences.

Thomas Schirrmacher, Richard Howell. Racism. With an essay on Caste in India. VKW: Bonn, 2011. 100 pp.

History and scientific errors of racism

Menschenrechte: Anspruch und Wirklichkeit. Holzgerlingen: SCM Hänssler, 2012. 120 pp.

[Human Rights]: Ethical arguments for human rights versus the present stage of the violation of human rights worldwide.

Christ and the Trinity in the Old Testament. Edited by James E. Anderson. RVB: Hamburg, 2013. 82 pp.

On Christ and the Trinity in the Old Testament and on 'the Angel of the Lord'. Taken from 'Ethik'.

Selection from the books edited by the author:

Scham- und Schuldorientierung in der Diskussion: Kulturanthropologische, missiologische und theologische Einsichten (mit Klaus W. Müller). VTR: Nürnberg & VKW: Bonn, 2006

[Shame- and Guiltorientation] A selection of experts from all continents on the difference between shame- and guiltoriented cultures and its implications for world missions.

HIV und AIDS als christliche Herausforderung (mit Kurt Bangert). Verlag für Kultur und Wissenschaft: Bonn, 2008. 211 pp.

[HIV and AIDS as Christian Challenge] Essay on how the Christian church should react to HIV and AIDS and how it does react. Published together with World Vision Germany.

Der Kampf gegen die weltweite Armut – Aufgabe der Evangelischen Allianz? Zur biblisch-theologischen Begründung der Micha-Initiative. (with Andreas Kusch). VKW/Idea: Bonn, 2009. 230 pp.

[The fight against poverty – task of the Evangelical Alliance?] Essays by theologians, missiologists, activists etc. in favour of the MICAH initiative of the World Evangelical Alliance.

Tough-Minded Christianity: Honoring the Legacy of John Warwick Montgomery. (with William Dembski). (2009) B&H Academic Publ.: Nashville (TN). 830 pp.

Large Festschrift with essays by many major Evangelical theologians and lawyers.

Calvin and World Mission: Essays- VKW: Bonn, VTR: Nürnberg, 2009. 204 pp.

Collection of essays from 1882 to 2002.

Biography

Prof. Dr. theol. Dr. phil. Thomas Schirrmacher, PhD, DD, (born 1960) is Ambassador for Human Rights of the World Evangelical Alliance, speaking for appr. 600 million Christians, chair of its Theological Commission, and director of its International Institute for Religious Freedom (Bonn, Cape Town, Colombo). He is also director of the Commission for Religious Freedom of the German and Austrian Evangelical Alliance. He is member of the board of the International Society for Human Rights.

Schirrmacher is professor of the sociology of religion at the State University of the West in Timisoara (Romania) and Distinguished Professor of Global Ethics and International Development at William Carey University in Shillong (Meghalaya, India). He is also president of 'Martin Bucer European Theological Seminary and Research Institutes' with small campuses in Bonn, Berlin, Zurich, Linz, Innsbruck, Prague, Istanbul, and Sao Paulo, where he teaches ethics and comparative religions.

He studied theology from 1978 to 1982 at STH Basel (Switzerland) and since 1983 Cultural Anthropology and Comparative Religions at Bonn State University. He earned a Drs. theol. in Missiology and Ecumenics at Theological University (Kampen/Netherlands) in 1984, and a Dr. theol. in Missiology and Ecumenics at Johannes Calvin Foundation (Kampen/Netherlands) in 1985, a Ph.D. in Cultural Anthropology at Pacific Western University in Los Angeles (CA) in 1989, a Th.D. in Ethics at Whitefield Theological Seminary in Lakeland (FL) in 1996, and a Dr. phil. in Comparative Religions / Sociology of Religion at State University of Bonn in 2007. In 1997 he received an honorary doctorate (D.D.) from Cranmer Theological House, in 2006 one from Acts University in Bangalore.

Schirrmacher regularly testifies in the German parliament and other parliaments in Europe, in the EU parliament in Brussels, the OSCE in Vienna and the UN Human Rights Council in Geneva.

He has written or edited 94 books on ethics, missiology and cultural anthropology, which were translated into 17 languages.

He is listed in Marquis' Who's Who in the World, Dictionary of International Biography, International Who is Who of Professionals, 2000 Outstanding Intellectuals of the 21st Century and many other biographical yearbooks.

See more at www.thomasschirrmacher.net/eine-seite/biography.

World Evangelical Alliance

World Evangelical Alliance is a global ministry working with local churches around the world to join in common concern to live and proclaim the Good News of Jesus in their communities. WEA is a network of churches in 129 nations that have each formed an evangelical alliance and over 100 international organizations joining together to give a worldwide identity, voice and platform to more than 600 million evangelical Christians. Seeking holiness, justice and renewal at every level of society – individual, family, community and culture, God is glorified and the nations of the earth are forever transformed.

Christians from ten countries met in London in 1846 for the purpose of launching, in their own words, "a new thing in church history, a definite organization for the expression of unity amongst Christian individuals belonging to different churches." This was the beginning of a vision that was fulfilled in 1951 when believers from 21 countries officially formed the World Evangelical Fellowship. Today, 150 years after the London gathering, WEA is a dynamic global structure for unity and action that embraces 600 million evangelicals in 129 countries. It is a unity based on the historic Christian faith expressed in the evangelical tradition. And it looks to the future with vision to accomplish God's purposes in discipling the nations for Jesus Christ.

Commissions:

- Theology
- Missions
- Religious Liberty
- Women's Concerns
- Youth
- Information Technology

Initiatives and Activities

- Ambassador for Human Rights
- Ambassador for Refugees
- Creation Care Task Force
- Global Generosity Network
- International Institute for Religious Freedom
- International Institute for Islamic Studies
- Leadership Institute
- Micah Challenge
- Global Human Trafficking Task Force
- Peace and Reconciliation Initiative
- UN-Team

Church Street Station
P.O. Box 3402
New York, NY 10008-3402
Phone +[1] 212 233 3046
Fax +[1] 646-957-9218
www.worldea.org

Giving Hands

GIVING HANDS GERMANY (GH) was established in 1995 and is officially recognized as a nonprofit foreign aid organization. It is an international operating charity that – up to now – has been supporting projects in about 40 countries on four continents. In particular we care for orphans and street children. Our major focus is on Africa and Central America. GIVING HANDS always mainly provides assistance for self-help and furthers human rights thinking.

The charity itself is not bound to any church, but on the spot we are co-operating with churches of all denominations. Naturally we also cooperate with other charities as well as governmental organizations to provide assistance as effective as possible under the given circumstances.

The work of GIVING HANDS GERMANY is controlled by a supervisory board. Members of this board are Manfred Feldmann, Colonel V. Doner and Kathleen McCall. Dr. Christine Schirrmacher is registered as legal manager of GIVING HANDS at the local district court. The local office and work of the charity are coordinated by Rev. Horst J. Kreie as executive manager. Dr. theol. Thomas Schirrmacher serves as a special consultant for all projects.

Thanks to our international contacts companies and organizations from many countries time and again provide containers with gifts in kind which we send to the different destinations where these goods help to satisfy elementary needs. This statutory purpose is put into practice by granting nutrition, clothing, education, construction and maintenance of training centers at home and abroad, construction of wells and operation of water treatment systems, guidance for self-help and transportation of goods and gifts to areas and countries where needy people live.

GIVING HANDS has a publishing arm under the leadership of Titus Vogt, that publishes human rights and other books in English, Spanish, Swahili and other languages.

These aims are aspired to the glory of the Lord according to the basic Christian principles put down in the Holy Bible.

Baumschulallee 3a • D-53115 Bonn • Germany
Phone: +49 / 228 / 695531 • Fax +49 / 228 / 695532
www.gebende-haende.de • info@gebende-haende.de

Martin Bucer Seminary

Faithful to biblical truth
Cooperating with the Evangelical Alliance
Reformed

Solid training for the Kingdom of God
- Alternative theological education
- Study while serving a church or working another job
- Enables students to remain in their own churches
- Encourages independent thinking
- Learning from the growth of the universal church.

Academic
- For the Bachelor's degree: 180 Bologna-Credits
- For the Master's degree: 120 additional Credits
- Both old and new teaching methods: All day seminars, independent study, term papers, etc.

Our Orientation:
- Complete trust in the reliability of the Bible
- Building on reformation theology
- Based on the confession of the German Evangelical Alliance
- Open for innovations in the Kingdom of God

Our Emphasis:
- The Bible
- Ethics and Basic Theology
- Missions
- The Church

Our Style:
- Innovative
- Relevant to society
- International
- Research oriented
- Interdisciplinary

Structure
- 15 study centers in 7 countries with local partners
- 5 research institutes
- President: Prof. Dr. Thomas Schirrmacher
  Vice President: Prof. Dr. Thomas K. Johnson
- Deans: Thomas Kinker, Th.D.;
  Titus Vogt, lic. theol., Carsten Friedrich, M.Th.

Missions through research
- Institute for Religious Freedom
- Institute for Islamic Studies
- Institute for Life and Family Studies
- Institute for Crisis, Dying, and Grief Counseling
- Institute for Pastoral Care

www.bucer.eu • info@bucer.eu
Berlin | Bielefeld | Bonn | Chemnitz | Hamburg | Munich | Pforzheim
Innsbruck | Istanbul | Izmir | Linz | Prague | São Paulo | Tirana | Zurich

www.ingramcontent.com/pod-product-compliance
Lightning Source LLC
Chambersburg PA
CBHW070323100426
42743CB00011B/2537